Slaying Dragons – *Prepare for Battle*
~~~
Applying the Wisdom of Exorcists to Your Spiritual Warfare

Slaying Dragons
-Prepare for Battle-

Applying the Wisdom of Exorcists to Your Spiritual Warfare

A
Companion Guide and Workbook
for
Slaying Dragons: What Exorcists See & What We Should Know

By Charles D. Fraune

Slaying Dragons Press

Copyright © 2022 by Charles D. Fraune. Slaying Dragons Press

First Edition 2022

ISBN: 9781735049755

Unless otherwise noted, all quotes from Sacred Scripture are from the Revised Standard Version of the Bible: Catholic Edition, copyright © 1965, 1966 the Division of Christian Education of the National Council of the Churches of Christ in the United States of America. Used by permission. All rights reserved.

Scripture quotes from the Douay-Rheims translation initialed as DR after the citation.

Prayers, unless clearly traditional or noted as *used with permission*, are original prayers by Charles D. Fraune.

All rights reserved. No part of this publication may be reproduced, stored in a retrieval system, or transmitted, in any form or by any means, electronic, mechanical, photocopying, recording, or otherwise, without the prior written permission of the publisher except for the use of brief quotations in a book review or scholarly journal.

Follow the author at *www.TheSlayingDragonsBook.com* for news, commentary, and publications on the topic of spiritual warfare. Shop for more books by this author and for related Catholic books and products at the website below. The author is available for talks at parishes and conferences. Use the "contact us" page at the website above or below to reach the author.

This book is also available in hardcover and spiral bound.

Slaying Dragons Press
www.TheRetreatBox.com

2022

Dedication

To Our Lady of Sorrows,
and to the glorious and triumphant Archangel,
Saint Michael.

St. Michael the Archangel,
defend us in battle.
Be our protection
against the wickedness and snares of the Devil.
May God rebuke him, we humbly pray,
and do thou,
O Prince of the heavenly hosts,
by the power of God,
cast into hell Satan, and all the evil spirits,
who prowl about the world
seeking the ruin of souls.
Amen.

Table of Contents

INTRODUCTION TO PREPARE FOR BATTLE 1

MY BATTLE PLAN 5

THE SPIRITUAL BATTLE 9

Part I

I: A HOLY LIFE 15
II: THE SERIOUSNESS OF SIN AND GRACE 29
III: PRAYERS AND DEVOTIONS 45
IV: GENERAL SPIRITUAL WARFARE 57
V: BEING STRATEGIC IN SPIRITUAL WARFARE 71
VI: OUR GUARDIAN ANGELS 85
VII: GRATITUDE FOR GOD'S PROTECTION 99
VIII: OUR THOUGHTS 111
IX: TEMPTATION 125
X: CONSIDERING EXTRAORDINARY PHENOMENA 139
XI: THE EFFECTS OF THE OCCULT 151
XII: THE MINISTRY OF THE EXORCIST 161

Part II

Prayers, Reflections, & Resources for Spiritual Purification & Renewal

SPIRITUAL WARFARE CHECKLIST 169
WHAT TO DO WITH OCCULT AND CURSED ITEMS 173
RENUNCIATION OF EVIL ACTIONS AND INFLUENCES 175
AN INTERIOR HEALING PROCESS 177
PROTOCOL FOR PRAYING TO BREAK THE FREEMASONIC CURSE 179
BINDING PRAYERS 183
CONSECRATION OF ONE'S EXTERIOR GOODS TO THE BLESSED VIRGIN MARY 185
THE ANGELIC WARFARE CONFRATERNITY 187

Powerful Prayers to Our Lord & Our Lady

LITANY OF THE MOST PRECIOUS BLOOD OF JESUS 193
NOVENA TO OUR LADY, UNDOER OF KNOTS 195
LITTLE ROSARY (OR CHAPLET) OF OUR LADY OF SORROWS 199
CHAPLET OF OUR LADY OF SORROWS 203
PRAYERS TO OUR LADY OF PERPETUAL SUCCOUR 207
REFLECTION – OUR LADY'S SUFFERING, LOVE, AND POWER 211

Prayers to Prepare the Soul for Spiritual Warfare

PRAYER FOR PERSEVERANCE IN THE STORM 217
A PRAYER TO END AN OPPRESSION 219
PRAYER TO ST. JOSEPH 221
PRAYER TO GUARDIAN ANGEL 223
ST. PATRICK'S BREASTPLATE 225
ACT OF FAITH 229
LITANY OF HUMILITY 231
PARENTAL BLESSING OF A CHILD 233
NOTES & JOURNALING 235
ABOUT THE AUTHOR 249

Introduction to Prepare for Battle

In my book, *Slaying Dragons: What Exorcists See & What We Should Know*, I presented the spiritual framework in which our Christian warfare take place. Demons are motivated by certain things, like hatred and envy. They seek to attack us in specific ways, through temptations crafted after careful observation of our habits. They are permitted to attack all men but are granted further entry into our lives through mortal sin and the occult. We have weapons to wield against them, such as the Sacraments, sacramentals, and an active prayer life.

After reading *Slaying Dragons*, the reader is equipped with the knowledge and counsel necessary to forge ahead in the spiritual life, and all the struggles it entails, with a confidence rooted in the fact that God is ever-present and all-powerful in our lives. The diabolical is ultimately unable to resist Him, or to work against the laws and commands He has established so as to limit their activity. As a result, we can find real peace in this life, albeit as a mere foretaste of that true peace which awaits us in Heaven.

In order to achieve this peace, there is real spiritual work that we must do. For many of us, we have accumulated wounds and spiritual baggage that make it difficult to persevere in prayer when life, and temptations, become a burden. Despite that, there is a power that Christ imparts, which we can receive, which will heal and liberate us, placing us again on the battlefield as properly trained soldiers.

The purpose of *Prepare for Battle* is to take the reader, who may or may not have read *Slaying Dragons*, into a personal journey of reflection regarding the state of the spiritual war in the reader's soul. The reflections in this book are broken up into themes, placed in the sections that make up the primary part of this guide. The sections are intended to lead the reader into a specific form of spiritual analysis that will refine his awareness of the strengths and weaknesses of his own spiritual warfare.

Many, after reading *Slaying Dragons*, have been left with a heart stirred to conversion and reform, ready to implement the many beneficial spiritual practices and wisdom which they learned about in that book. However, many also do not know where to go next with that knowledge. That is the intent of *Prepare for Battle*: to take Christian souls deeper into their spiritual warfare training, by guiding them toward an understanding of what still needs to be done in order to have the proper strength for the battle to which God has called them.

The thematic reflections in the book focus on what the reader personally needs to remember, implement, analyze, and reform in his life. The book covers not only the intellectual reform the reader will need to undertake, but also the spiritual and devotional work which he may have come to see has been lacking in his life.

How to Use *Prepare for Battle*

Each *Section* presented for reflection on a Theme will include the following elements:
- A unique prayer aligned with that Theme
- An introduction to the Theme
- Verses from Sacred Scripture that focus on the importance of that Theme, as well as summaries of the verses and questions for reflection
- A brief *Ponderance* on the Theme and its connection to spiritual warfare and salvation
- Selected reminders from the Compendium sections of *Slaying Dragons* and questions to consider
- A number of *Considerations* and *Action Items*, each with space to write notes
- Additional pages for notetaking
- A unique prayer on the Theme to close the reflection.

When reading through the *Sections,* make a note of issues and reflections that especially stand out to you. Since everyone is at a different point in their spiritual journey, some questions in the book will be very relevant to certain people, while not pertaining to others. Keep moving forward if an individual consideration or suggested reflection does not present itself as a necessary issue for your spiritual analysis.

Prepare for Battle can be approached in a variety of ways. However, this guide is not intended to be read straight through, nor meant to be read through at a quick pace. Having qualities similar to an examination of conscience, the book will require the reader to dedicate time, effort, concentration, and reflection for it to bear the intended fruit in the soul.

- **APPROACH I**
    - **Each *Section* over a series of days (or weeks), such as:**
        - *Day 1: Prayer and Scripture*
        - *Day 2: Ponderance and Consideration*
        - *Day 3: Pick a memory verse from the Scriptures listed and read the provided reminders from* Slaying Dragons.
        - *Day 4: Action Items*
            - *Some of these may take longer to fully process than others. Avoid rushing through them to get to the next one. Perhaps read one in the morning and let it sit with you throughout the day. Pick a good time to speak to Our Lord about it and journal or make a plan to fulfill any new holy desires it has stirred.*
        - *Day 5-7: Journal and Review and Prayer*
- **APPROACH II**
    - Read the Prayer of a chosen *Section* every day and work at your own pace through that *Section*.
    - Note the Resources in PART II and use as beneficial along the way.
    - When you finish that *Section*, move on to the one that appeals to you the most.

- **APPROACH III**
    o Use *Prepare for Battle* as part of a Catholic study group, men's or women's group, or parish prayer group.

Reading *Slaying Dragons* is important in order to fully utilize and understand this manual. One who is well-versed in spiritual warfare wisdom could pick up *Prepare for Battle* and make good use of it. However, *Prepare for Battle* is built from the many insights that are compiled in *Slaying Dragons* and the use of both books together will bring the greatest impact.

It is also advisable to use a spiritual journal along with *Prepare for Battle*. Though there is a lot of space provided within this book for writing, the reader may prefer to use a separate writing space. Further, *Prepare for Battle* will help initiate a deeper recollection on the spiritual life and make the use of a spiritual journal very helpful for continued growth.

There are many Scripture verses presented throughout the book. Read them thoughtfully and take note of the ones that jump out, impress you, or address a thought or issue that is on your mind that day. Consider using the ones that stand out as key verses to remember: memorize them, write them out, and place them where you see it regularly. Some ideal areas to place these include a bathroom mirror, dining room table, near the coffee pot, on your computer screen, or near the cup holder in your car.

Resources in PART II

The second part of the book is filled with important resources. Many of these are beneficial to all who read this book, while others, like the *Protocol to Break the Freemasonic Curse*, will only be needed by those who have Freemasonry in their family.

The Appendices are broken up into sections:
- *Prayers and Reflections for Spiritual Purification and Renewal*
- *Powerful Prayers to Our Lord and Our Lady*
- *Prayers to Prepare the Soul for Spiritual Warfare*

The first section contains very useful tools for evaluating what is needed in the work of fortifying your soul. These include, *Spiritual Warfare Checklist, What to Do with Occult and Cursed Items,* and, among others, *An Interior Healing Process*.

The second section includes prayers and devotions highly recommended by the great Saints, Our Lord and Our Lady, and, of course, exorcists. This includes *Litany of the Precious Blood, Novena to Our Lady, Undoer of Knots,* and two versions of the *Chaplet of Our Lady of Sorrows*.

The third section contains several additional spiritual warfare and classic prayers, such as *A Prayer for Perseverance in the Storm, St. Patrick's Breastplate,* and *Parental Blessing of a Child*.

Space to Write

Throughout the book, and also at the end, is plenty of space to write and make notes. While it is recommended that the reader consider using a separate journal, the available space for writing may be sufficient. One approach, similar to an aspect of *An Interior Healing Process*[1], is to write about certain deep spiritual things on a separate sheet of paper where, after presenting them to Our Lord, they can be burned as a part of letting go of past evils or entrusting an aspect of your spiritual life to His special care and Providence.

> *"Be you humbled therefore under the mighty hand of God,*
> *that he may exalt you in the time of visitation:*
> *Casting all your care upon him,*
> *for he hath care of you."*
> ~
> *1 Peter 5:6-7 DR*

---

[1] Page 177

My Battle Plan

A war does not end after only one battle – a Christian's spiritual battle is the same. We should be prepared to create many battle plans in order to move forward in our journey toward the final battle at the moment of our passing from this life.

As you work through *Slaying Dragons Prepare for Battle*, keep in mind the following Battle Plan template. Its purpose is to help you construct a fruitful approach to achieving specific spiritual goals. There are many aspects of the spiritual life that must be taken into consideration as you navigate this journey to eternity. This template will give you the structure for a successful endeavor.

St. Martin of Tours, a solider on the battlefield both physically and spiritually, fought with the devil his whole life. At his death, the devil attempted to lead him to ruin, but he was not deceived, for he had spent sufficient time fighting the devil and knew the tricks that would be used against him. If we, in imitation of this great Saint, similarly engage in constant and calculated spiritual warfare throughout life, the Enemy of our souls will not catch us off our guard and vulnerable at the end.

A blank version of this template is available on my website.[1]

~~~~~~~

My Goal:

What is the goal of this specific battle? What spiritual good are you seeking?

My Enemies:

What are the known weaknesses that are preventing me from reaching this goal?

Work through the Sections in <u>Slaying Dragons – Prepare for Battle</u> that correspond with one or more of these weaknesses or challenges.

My War Cry:

Pick a psalm or song to memorize and use as your "war cry," or song of inspiration and strength, during this focused time. Keep this in mind as you read through the Scriptures in each Section.

---

[1] www.TheSlayingDragonsBook.com

Slaying Dragons – Prepare for Battle

My Fellow Soldiers:

Think about or research a Saint whose intercession you can seek in your battle. Consider researching a Saint who is related to your goal or your weakness, or a saint who has been on your mind lately.

Battle Time Prayer:

Write a unique prayer that includes binding prayers, the Saint whose intercession you are seeking, and the title for Our Lady that stands out the most, to help you reach your goal and overcome your weaknesses. If you are not comfortable writing a prayer, find one that is fitting and consider adding the binding prayer at the end. As you progress through <u>Slaying Dragons – Prepare for Battle</u>, *note the prayers that stood out to you and use these, or parts of them, to help craft your prayer.*

Actions:

What concrete actions need to be done to reach your goal or overcome your weaknesses? Think of prayer, fasting, almsgiving, and other forms of penance, and specific aspects of the Faith which you need to learn more about through reading or doing research. Think of actions that promote the virtue which is the opposite of your main vices.

Practicalities:

Return to the above actions and, with specific days and times in mind, list when you will accomplish these things, how frequently, for how long, and in what order. If time is a limiting factor, then consider what you can do to overcome that? When will you find time for prayer, the most needed thing, each day?

Physical and psychological challenges during this battle:

List any known physical or psychological challenges you will likely face or currently face. Think of the medicines you take and how they could impact you during this effort. Consider how you will maintain or improve your physical and mental health during this battle. Consider whether you need to consult with a physician or counselor before enacting a more challenging battle plan.

Relationships:

Think of how you will maintain important and necessary relationships during this time, such as relationships with family members, friends, etc. What can you do to make sure any sacrifices you make don't become penances for other people? Are there any people who can help you during this journey, like a spiritual director or mentor, and, if so, how and when can you meet with them?

Other obstacles that you foresee:

As you begin this specific battle, think of any or all obstacles you expect to emerge and how you will try to overcome them.

Planned starting date:

Pick a good date to begin, such as the feast day of a Saint who is dear to you, or some other day that adds an important significance to initiating the Battle Plan.

Temptation to discouragement:

If you reach a point where you feel like you have failed or are failing, what are the spiritual weapons, prayers, techniques, images, friends, conversations with others, etc., you will use to help summon the courage to try again.

Obstacles noted along the way:

List these here and either come up with ways to overcome them or list ideas to do so. Make sure you are journaling along the way so you remember how everything unfolded and progressed.

Wisdom at the End of the Battle:

At the end of the battle, when your spiritual life improves, list the things you have learned, or the practices you want to continue, and pick a new goal to further your spiritual growth, and what the next Battle Plan needs to look like.

Signature:

Consider signing your name in a more solemn manner, invoking the assistance of Our Lord, Our Lady, or your Guardian Angel. You could sign the Battle Plan after the manner of the Consecration to Jesus through Mary, stating, "I, _____, a faithless sinner, do hereby petition the grace of the Holy Trinity to fulfill this Battle Plan and to progress in my conformity to Our Lord Jesus Christ."

_____

The Spiritual Battle

Our Christian life is one of warfare. To the one who has read *Slaying Dragons: What Exorcists See & What We Should Know*, this concept is crystal clear.

However, our main battle is not against the extraordinary manifestations of the demons but against the subtle, crafty, calculated, insidious, and tireless efforts of the Evil One to take our gaze off of Christ. It is against the storms and waves which Satan has stirred up in this world in order to frighten and overtake us.

Peter, with the power of faith, walked across the stormy sea to come to Jesus, but his faith was not steadfast, and he faltered. As the Gospel of Matthew states, "But the boat in the midst of the sea was tossed with the waves: for the wind was contrary... [and] seeing the wind strong, he was afraid: and when he began to sink, he cried out, saying: 'Lord, save me'."[1]

Though here we see what may be, in the wind and the waves, a manifestation of Satan's desire to harm Christ and the Apostles, it was the *internal* attack which caused Peter to falter. His bravery made it so that the wind and waves did not frighten him, but his unenduring faith caused him to look away from Christ and sink beneath them.

Our Lord says, "If you have faith as a grain of mustard seed, you could say to this sycamine tree, 'Be rooted up, and be planted in the sea,' and it would obey you... [and] you will say to this mountain, 'Move from hence to yonder place,' and it will move; and nothing will be impossible to you."[2] Likewise, when the Apostles struggle to cast out a demon and are ultimately unable to do so, Our Lord rebukes them for their "little faith."[3]

Faith, then, is the central power in the spiritual battle. St. Paul says, "In all things taking the shield of faith, wherewith you may be able to extinguish all the fiery darts of the most wicked one."[4] This is the only element of the "armor of God" which is stated to be used "in all things" or "above all."[5]

St. Thomas Aquinas states, in his commentary on Ephesians 6, that "faith is presupposed to all the other virtues just as a shield is basic to all weapons." He continues, saying

> "Just as a shield wards off the arrows, so faith repels what is aimed against it and gains the victory. The saints 'by faith conquered kingdoms'[6] [The fiery darts] are

---

[1] Matthew 14:24,30 DR
[2] Luke 17:6 and Matthew 17:20
[3] Matthew 17:20
[4] Ephesians 6:16 DR
[5] RSVCE translation
[6] Hebrews 11:33

extinguished through faith; it quenches present and transitory temptations with the eternal and spiritual blessings promised in Holy Scripture."[7]

Entanglement in Evil

In this world, the faith of many falters and grows weak. As the Apostles experienced in the Sea of Galilee, we are up against a tide of evil that seems to rise every day. The sources of temptation, celebrations of sin, and invitations to the occult abound in our world. We are at a time where, it seems, none can escape this bombardment, but by a truly heroic effort.

Thus, our warfare is, perhaps, unique when compared with the previous ages of the Church. Our battle consists of a daily assault on our virtues and our faith in Christ, not through threats of martyrdom but through the slow and steady pressure of coercion to compromise. Apostasy lies in wait as the culture around us descends deep into infidelity and opposition to Our Lord.

Therefore, to steel our wills and furnish our souls with the proper armor, we must each address a wide array of issues to ensure the Enemy has not found kinks, cracks, or gaps in our armor, which he intends to exploit. We must not let ourselves be like King Théoden at his fortress, the Hornburg in Helm's Deep, proud of his fortifications yet oblivious to the one weakness in the defenses which his enemy knew so well. Indeed, his enemy knew the weakness and Théoden was completely unaware, such that the war against him brought a sudden and nearly fatal calamity.[8]

Our Enemy is wiser and more aware than Théoden's, but we also have the wisdom and power of the Holy Spirit and the Church of Jesus Christ to illuminate our minds and strengthen our wills, that we may not be caught off guard and permit the Enemy to sneak in with his devastation.

Fortifying the Castle of the Soul

This book is a battle plan and a guide, that the reader may more thoroughly *Prepare for Battle* and be victorious.

Take this work of faith and holiness seriously. Search the garden of your soul for all the hidden weeds and remove them. Leave no stone unturned in your search for the sources of discord and discontent. Ask the Holy Spirit to guide you onto a path of purification and renewal, to place within your hands a renewed sword of the Spirit, and to shine the light of His love into all the hidden regions of your being, that you may more quickly and more completely grow "to mature manhood, to the measure of the stature of the fulness of Christ."[9]

---

[7] Commentary on St. Paul's Epistle to the Ephesians https://isidore.co/aquinas/SSEph.htm
[8] King Théoden is a fictional character from the epic book, *Lord of the Rings*, by Catholic author J.R.R. Tolkien. Théoden's enemy knew of a weakness in the outer wall defending the city and planted an explosive there which unexpectedly decimated the defenses.
[9] Ephesians 4:13

Do not give in to discouragement or disappointment as you reflect on your wounds, weaknesses, failures, and shortcomings. These are the means by which Christ can meet you with His redemptive work, and the places in your soul where He can fill you with His grace. Keep in mind the many terrible sinners who were transformed, through awareness, humility, penance, and spiritual battle, into some of the mightiest warriors in Our Lord's army.

For the goal of the life of the Christian is this,
> "That we may no longer be children, tossed to and fro and carried about with every wind of doctrine, by the cunning of men, by their craftiness in deceitful wiles. Rather, speaking the truth in love, we are to grow up in every way into him who is the head, into Christ, from whom the whole body, joined and knit together by every joint with which it is supplied, when each part is working properly, makes bodily growth and upbuilds itself in love."[10]

A Reflection on Heaven

Let us set our minds clearly on the goal: the glory of Heaven. With our minds filled with a concrete hope regarding the promises of Almighty God, we will go into the battle with boldness and courage and be less inclined to follow after the petty gifts and offerings from the world, the flesh, and the devil.

The following reflection is from *Introduction to the Devout Life*, where St. Frances de Sales calls us to imagine the glory of Heaven. The images he presents and the sentiments he stirs are vital for us to immerse ourselves into. In this world, we struggle with our affections and desires, keeping them pure and balanced by reason and grace, not letting them lead us away from God and toward an idolatry of creatures. Holy affections and holy desires, such as are kindled by reflections on the beauty of Heaven, inflame the soul with a deep and powerful longing for God. This longing, fueled by grace, can be a great comfort and encouragement along the way.

~~~

> "1. Consider a fair and clear night, and reflect how delightful it is to behold the sky bespangled with all that multitude and variety of stars; then join this beautiful sight with that of a fine day, so that the brightness of the sun may not prevent the clear view of the stars nor of the moon; and then say boldly that all this beauty put together is nothing when compared with the excellence of the great heavenly paradise. O how lovely, how desirable is this place! O how precious is this city!

> "2. Consider the glory, the beauty, and the multitude of the inhabitants of this happy country; millions of millions of angels, of cherubin and seraphin; choirs of apostles, prophets, martyrs, confessors, virgins, and holy women; the multitude is innumerable. O how glorious is this company! the least of them is more beautiful to behold than the whole world; what a sight then will it be to behold them all! But, O

---
[10] Ephesians 4:14-16

my God! how happy are they! they sing incessantly harmonious songs of eternal love! they always enjoy a state of felicity; they mutually give each other unspeakable contentment, and live in the consolation of a happy, indissoluble society.

"3. In fine, consider how happy the blessed are in the enjoyment of God, who favors them forever with a sight of his lovely presence, and thereby infuses into their hearts a treasure of delights. How great a felicity must it be to be united to their first principle, their Sovereign Good. They are like happy birds, flying and singing perpetually in the air of his divinity, which encompasses them on all sides with incredible pleasure. There every one does his utmost, and sings without envy the praises of his Creator. Blessed be thou forever, O sweet and sovereign Creator and Saviour, who art so good, and who dost communicate to us so liberally the everlasting treasures of thy glory! And blessed forever be you, says he, my beloved creatures, who have served me so faithfully, with love and constancy; behold you shall be admitted to sing my praises forever."[11]

~~~

This is the promise of eternal life. This is the great treasure which countless Saints have understood to be worthy of pursuit by laying aside all that this world offers. This longing for the glory and beauty and eternal Love of God led them to undertake all that is required of us that we might merit to enter into that abode. Let the Holy Spirit convict you, stir you to greater spiritual work, and set your heart unshakable on His courts.

---

[11] St. Frances de Sales, *Introduction to a Devout Life*, pg. 40-41 (archive.org)

Part I

I: A Holy Life

Patron Saint: St. Benedict

~PRAYER~

Eternal Father,
I thank Thee for my life
and I offer it again to Thee this day.
Bestow Thy grace upon me
sufficient to call my soul, at all times, to reflect on Thy holy love.
Make me desire, by Thy grace,
to live for Heaven above all
and to no longer have any cares for this world,
for all is passing away.
Make me desire to cling to Thee always
by ever seeking to be pleasing to Thee.
Amen.

~INTRODUCTION~

Holiness of life is the fundamental power of our spiritual warfare. It is the consequence of a relationship with Our Lord, one nurtured through a true friendship, protected by obedience, and enlivened by trust in Divine Providence. When a person is considering whether or not he is doing what is necessary to protect his soul from evil and to ensure he is faithfully following the promptings of the Holy Spirit, the question of the holiness of his soul is paramount.

"Am I fulfilling the Lord's commands? Do I seek to excel in virtue and charity? Do I cherish prayer and allow it to be the core of each new day I am given?" These are the questions which will indicate whether the grace of God is flowing and active in his soul. If these are being fulfilled, the man's soul is truly set on the right path. This is not the end, though, for wisdom, counsel, and knowledge are also required to ensure his path does not go astray.

Holiness of life depends, as St. Cyprian states, on avoiding occasions of sin after embarking on a holy life. For the devil, once driven out of the soul, waits for a moment of weakness. It is, as St. Alphonsus says, like Lazarus, who, though he rose once from the dead, still died again. So we are if we do not fortify the life of holiness: risen in Christ, yet at risk of dying again.[1]

---

[1] St. Alphonsus Liguori, *Preparation for Death*, 320

Reflections on Sacred Scripture
The following Scripture verses relate to the theme of this section. Read through them slowly, noticing what stands out in each passage. Does a verse convict you of something you are lacking? Does a verse confirm that you are being faithful, thus clearing away doubts? Does a verse strike your heart with a new understanding of God and His holy will?

~~~

~MATTHEW 5:48~
You, therefore, must be perfect, as your heavenly Father is perfect.

~1 PETER 1:14-16~
As obedient children, do not be conformed to the passions of your former ignorance, but as he who called you is holy, be holy yourselves in all your conduct; ^since^ it is written, "You shall be holy, for I am holy."

~2 CORINTHIANS 7:1~
Since we have these promises, beloved, let us cleanse ourselves from every defilement of body and spirit, and make holiness perfect in the fear of God.

~HEBREWS 12:14~
Strive for peace with all men, and for the holiness without which no one will see the Lord.

~PSALM 119:9~
How can a young man keep his way pure? By guarding it according to thy word.

~PHILIPPIANS 2:14-15~
Do all things without grumbling or questioning, that you may be blameless and innocent, children of God without blemish in the midst of a crooked and perverse generation, among whom you shine as lights in the world.

~ROMANS 6:22~
But now that you have been set free from sin and have become slaves of God, the return you get is sanctification and its end, eternal life.

~MATTHEW 6:33~
But seek first his kingdom and his righteousness, and all these things shall be yours as well.

From the Scriptures:
- Our holiness is tied to our configuration to Christ, the Image of the Father.
- God, who is holy, calls us to imitate Him, and to be holy as He is holy, in the manner He has revealed through His Son. This requires us to leave behind our former manner of living, as it was carried out without divine wisdom, and was simply servitude to our fallen nature.

A Holy Life

- To achieve holiness, we must avoid all sin and spiritual defilement, binding ourselves to the truth that there are rewards and consequences to our actions as members of the New Covenant. If we desire to see God eternally in Heaven, we must fulfill this call to holiness.
- We must nurture a deep trust and surrender to God in order to steadfastly seek that which is right, not turning our heads or inclining our ears to the maxims of this fallen world.
- When we set our sights on Heaven, and pursue righteousness above all else, we will reap the benefits of sanctification, and grow in grace toward eternal life.

As you begin crafting your spiritual warfare Battle Plan, take a moment to process the above verses, and where they may have convicted you about the current status of your fervor for holiness.

1. Do I really believe that I am called to union with God and to resemble Him in holiness?
2. Have I made a real break with the sinful ways of my past and those which the world loves?
3. Am I truly dedicated to works of righteousness, trusting that God's commands are for my good, or do I still present a divided heart when I offer Him my prayers and actions each day?

_____
_____
_____
_____
_____
_____
_____
_____
_____
_____
_____
_____
_____
_____
_____
_____

Slaying Dragons – Prepare for Battle

A Holy Life

~PONDERANCE~

Holiness of life is the goal of human existence. This is the reason we were created. This is the criteria for our Judgment at death. This determines whether we are happy in this life and whether we will be happy with God forever in the life to come.

Nurturing holiness of life is like tending a garden such that the soil is rich and life-giving. A holy life leads to the blossoming of all virtues, the ordering of life, the freedom to pursue the supreme good, and the distribution of grace to all with whom we come in contact.

Holiness of life is a power. It enables us, by God's gift, to intercede for others and call down grace from Heaven, to change and move hearts, to persevere to the end in the face of adversity, to desire God with an insatiable love, and to resist and block and drive away the diabolical forces intent on robbing us of all the good which God has imparted to us.

Holiness of life is also a quality of being which actively changes us into children of God, human beings who are transformed into the Image of Christ, the Son of God. It involves a death to our old selves and, through this negation of a love for the world, a rising in Christ to a life which can only be fulfilled by entrance into Heaven.

Becoming holy means becoming someone whose heart is no longer divided by a dual interest, that of worldly pleasure and that of eternal delights. The man who is becoming holy is the man who is losing interest in the goods of this earth, placing them among the lesser things while God, and all that pertains to Him, takes center stage in his mind and in his will.

In the Book of Genesis, we read of Jacob's vision of a ladder to Heaven. It says, "And he dreamed that there was a ladder set up on the earth, and the top of it reached to heaven; and behold, the angels of God were ascending and descending on it!"[2] St. Frances de Sales says that this ladder gives "a true picture of the devout life." He says, "The two sides between which we climb upward, and to which the rungs are fastened, represent prayer, which calls down God's love, and the sacraments, which confer it. The rungs are the various degrees of charity by which we ascend from virtue to virtue, either descending by deeds of help and support for our neighbor or, by contemplation, ascending to a loving union with God."

The devout life, then, is the life that leads us, by acts of devotion, deep prayer, and reliance upon the Sacraments, up the ladder which Christ brought down in His Incarnation. It is this ladder which, in His Ascension, He strengthened, for, as St. Paul adds, "When he ascended on high he led a host of captives, and he gave gifts to men."[3]

---

[2] Genesis 28:12
[3] Ephesians 4:8

A reminder of some essential points, from *Slaying Dragons*...

+ It is important to be honest about our weaknesses and to seek the healing of our past and our vices in order to proceed more steadily in the spiritual life.
+ Allowing Our Lord to heal us, and remaining obedient to Him at all times, will obtain for us the strength we require.
+ Demons attach themselves to people, things, and places when disorder is introduced. This includes abuse and trauma. These are grave wounds which the demons seek to exploit.
+ Demons observe and study us but cannot see our thoughts. They build their attacks around our weaknesses and wounds.
+ The best way to combat diabolical obsession is humility and mental prayer.
+ St. Louis de Montfort says that the humble servants of Mary, in union with her, will crush the head of Satan with their humility.
+ According to St. Louis de Montfort, it is the humility of Mary which humiliates the devil more than the power of God, which is why the devil fears her "in a certain sense more than God himself."[4]
+ Demons cannot tolerate nor endure humility in a soul.
+ The Blessed Virgin Mary gained, through her humility, what Satan lost through his pride.

Questions to consider:
- Have I become so used to my weaknesses, even small ones, that I no longer notice them as obstacles to holiness?
- Am I humble enough to admit to Christ that I have failed Him throughout my life and need Him to apply His medicinal grace to the wounds my sins have caused?
- Have I taken an aggressive approach to ridding myself of evil and indulgent and self-centered inclinations that are the primary motivators to committing sins?
- Do I really understand what it means to be humble, such that I imitate Our Lord and Our Lady and make myself less assailable by the Enemy?

___

[4] St. Louis de Montfort, *True Devotion*, 52. This does not mean Mary is more powerful than God, but that her status as a creature, yet with full power, leads Satan to fear being conquered by her. She conquers his pride through her humility, which is intolerable to Satan.

A Holy Life

Slaying Dragons – Prepare for Battle

~CONSIDERATIONS~

#1. Are there any clear divisions in your life, such as when you do not speak to someone, or refuse to visit someone, or ignore them in your heart, who is a member of your family or otherwise is in your life to a certain extent? These divisions weigh on the soul and can be exploited by the diabolical. What is one way you can begin to resolve these divisions, even if that resolution is one-sided, due to the inability to speak to the other person about it?
- Whom are you separated from?
- Who is the one who bears the blame, in all honesty?
- What can be done to heal the division, if only in the heart and not through communications?
- What prayers will you offer with the intention of healing this division?

_____
_____
_____
_____
_____
_____

#2. Consider how smart the demons are and how much they know. Remember, though, from their example, that smarts and intellectual prowess will not merit for anyone the Beatific Vision. Only goodness, grace, and holiness will do that.
- Where in your life do you place your intellectual abilities above the power of purity, humility, and surrender to Divine Providence?
- Do you consider yourself to be without a strong mind? If so, does this frustrate you or aid you to be humble, since God has granted you this simplicity?
- How well do you surrender your intellectual strengths or weaknesses to the Lord in thanksgiving for giving it to you as a gift?

_____
_____
_____
_____
_____
_____
_____

A Holy Life

#3. The devil cannot stand, and runs away from, humility. Would you say you are a humble person? Would your friends agree? Would the devil agree?
- Take a break in some fashion, like a walk or sitting on the porch in silence. What does your conscience tell you about the state of your soul on this question? Are you really a proud person and you just don't admit to it? Think about how people act around you. Do they ever react to you in ways that would reveal that you have a prideful way about you?
- Think about whether you do any of the following:
    o ridicule others or put them down in conversation, compare people's statements to similar ones which were made by obviously ignorant people,
    o highlight another person's mistakes at a moment when your own are being noticed,
    o deflect from your own error by shifting all of the blame to someone else who merely shared in the same mistake in a small manner
- People who are proud often overlook the suffering of people right around them. Are you sensitive to the sufferings of others and eager to be compassionate toward them?
    o If you see that it is necessary, what concrete action can you start including, today, in order to be more humble?

_____
_____
_____
_____
_____
_____
_____
_____
_____
_____

#4. Demons have relationships among themselves, but these are animated by hatred, wrath, humiliation, ridicule, and domination. Demons also seek to instill these same attitudes into us and destroy us through bad friendships. Good friendships, however, can be a powerful source of consolation, conversion, and the increase of virtue and spiritual zeal.
Reflect on the kind of friendships that you have.
- Are you tolerating negative friendships?
- Are you selective about your friends?
- Do you feel bound to endure mistreatment from your friends in order to simply have "friends" in your life?
- Do you demonstrate the care you have for your friends with a Christ-like love?

- How can you show a friend that you care for them this week? Are you prudently taking opportunities to treat your friends with the Christ-like love that we have been given?

_____
_____
_____
_____
_____
_____
_____
_____
_____
_____
_____
_____

#5. Fasting is a powerful spiritual weapon, but in this decadent and materialistic culture, where food is in plenty and great variety, it is often difficult to give up snacking, meat, and sweet things, and especially an entire meal. However, fasting places a crucial role in the spiritual life and in the work of resisting, and casting out, the diabolical.
In your spiritual life, how important of a place does fasting hold?
- Look at your weekly routine.
- See if you can pick two days where you can either avoid all snacks and/or skip a meal altogether.
- If you are unable to fast due to a significant medical condition, consider other areas where you can fast (technology, certain foods, laziness, etc.).
- Remember to offer it up as a spiritual sacrifice for a specific intention.[5]

_____
_____
_____
_____

---

[5] It is important to remember that, in the traditional life of the Church across the centuries, fasting has held a central and frequent place. Today, the modern practice is very lax, but this is not an inspiration of the Holy Spirit: it reflects a lack of faith.

A Holy Life

_____

_____

_____

_____

_____

#6. Get into the routine of making a regular examination of conscience. Ask the Blessed Mother and St. Joseph to intercede for you to help you see your sins and faults, be fully contrite, and renounce them. Make a more concerted effort to do a thorough examination before going to Confession. The more deeply your contrition goes, the more deeply grace can travel into your soul.
- There are many good Examinations of Conscience. Find one that fits your age and state in life the best. Check my website for a good list.[6]
- Do an examination of Conscience each night before bed.
- Consider keeping a journal and noting the sins and vices you are noticing.
- Look for a pattern and then adjust your penitential and spiritual life accordingly.
- Take sin seriously.

#7. Central to the fall of the demons was a prideful rejection of God's plan. When we push against God's will or grumble beneath the weight of the Cross in our lives, we must remember that we are taking part in this same rebellion, albeit in a less severe way. When you notice this resistance in your will, pray the Our Father slowly, dwelling on the words, "Thy will be done."
- If you are struggling with accepting a cross that Our Lord has given you, consider the power of gratitude. Take time each day to be grateful for the blessings Our Lord has bestowed on you. Try to do this from the first moment you arise in the morning: be grateful for food, water, housing, clothes, employment, friends, etc.

#8. Are there any doctrines of the Church which you hold in suspicion, reject, criticize, or to which you otherwise project an attitude of resistance and insubordination? If so, think carefully about your motives.
- What are the teachings of the Church that you struggle to accept or outright reject?
- What is the source for this hesitation to trust Our Lord on this teaching?
- Meditate on how the rejection of a single doctrine of the Faith is an act of pride and a sign that you lack the supernatural virtue of faith, as St. Thomas teaches.
- Was it by a bad example on the part of another that pushed you to reject this doctrine?
- Or was it the result of a sin you once committed, which now motivates you to push against something Our Lord has revealed?
- Or is there another reason?

---

[6] www.TheSlayingDragonsBook.com

Slaying Dragons – Prepare for Battle

A Holy Life

~ADDITIONAL NOTES FOR THIS SECTION~

Slaying Dragons – Prepare for Battle

~PRAYER~

Bestow upon me, O God,
grace in abundance,
Thy very life and holiness,
that my mind and my heart may be sanctified,
that my decisions and my desires be made pure,
that my pride may be crushed,
and that my hope would rest in Thee alone.
Take up Thy dwelling within me
and move me by Thy love
that, propelled by the consolation of Thy love and Truth,
I may lay down my earthly life,
with its cares and passing glories,
and take hold of Thy glorious Hand,
to lead me to eternal delights.
Amen.

II: The Seriousness of Sin and Grace

Patron Saint: St. Augustine

~PRAYER~

A clean heart create in me, O God,
and a new and right spirit place within me,
that I may hold fast to Thy ways
and not stray from Thy commands.
For the Enemy pursues my soul,
he is quick to come against me,
knowing my ways and the weaknesses of my steps.
Cast me not from Thy presence, O God,
according to what my sins deserve,
but look upon me,
clinging to the pierced Feet of Thy Son,
whose Blood I adore as the price
paid for my redemption.
Beneath Thy shelter,
and the mantle of the Mother of Thy Son,
I shall surely stay on the path of salvation
and, with steady feet, trample the Enemy as I proceed.
Amen.

~INTRODUCTION~

St. Frances de Sales states, "Although all the Israelites left Egypt in effect, not all of them left in affection, and hence in the wilderness many of them regretted their lack of the onions and fleshpots of Egypt. In like manner, there are penitents who leave sin in effect, but do not leave it in affection. They resolve never to sin again, but it is with a certain reluctance that they give up or abstain from the fatal delights of sin. Their heart renounces and shuns sin but looks back at it just as Lot's wife looked back at Sodom."[1]

Our earthly existence is a time of judging rightly the value of sin and grace. In this life, we are tested abundantly and our allegiance wavers from one to the other. In our weakness, we often do not have a single master, but constantly betray one while turning to follow the other. We must take this matter seriously, for, at the moment of our death, one allegiance will be eternal.

---

[1] St. Frances de Sales, *Introduction to the Devout Life*, p. 50

Reflections on Sacred Scripture
The following Scripture verses relate to the theme of this section. Read through them slowly, noticing what stands out in each passage. Does a verse convict you of something you are lacking? Does a verse confirm that you are being faithful, thus clearing away doubts? Does a verse strike your heart with a new understanding of God and His holy will?

~~~

~JOHN 3:5~
Truly, truly, I say to you, unless one is born of water and the Spirit, he cannot enter the kingdom of God.

~LUKE 13:3~
No; but unless you repent you will all likewise perish.

~MATTHEW 5:29~
If your right eye causes you to sin, pluck it out and throw it away; it is better that you lose one of your members than that your whole body be thrown into hell.

~ MATTHEW 12:45~
Then he goes and brings with him seven other spirits more evil than himself, and they enter and dwell there; and the last state of that man becomes worse than the first.

~GALATIANS 5:21~ (cf. 1 Cor. 6:9; Eph 5:5)
I warn you, as I warned you before, that those who do such things shall not inherit the kingdom of God.

~ GALATIANS 5:22-24~
But the fruit of the Spirit is love, joy, peace, patience, kindness, goodness, faithfulness, [gentleness], self-control; against such there is no law.

~1 CORINTHIANS 9: 26-27~
Well, I do not run aimlessly, I do not box as one beating the air; [but] I pommel my body and subdue it, lest after preaching to others I myself should be disqualified.

From the Scriptures:
- The grace of God through Baptism is necessary if we hope to attain to eternal life.
- God is merciful and patient, but He will punish us in justice if we persevere in sin.
- There is no pain, nor torture, nor sacrifice in this life that comes close to the misery of Hell. All that is disagreeable here must be endured, for the crown of glory is truly worth it all.
- We must not lay down our sword, nor cease our labors, nor look back upon the pleasures of sin left behind, for in that moment, the demons are ready and permitted to launch a more vicious attack, should we fail in our resolve to follow Our Lord and take up the Cross daily.
- There are some sins that will, if we continue in them until death, exclude us from Heaven.

The Seriousness of Sin and Grace

- Learn the revealed signs that the Holy Spirit is alive in the soul and seek to nurture these.
- Even the man most gifted in grace must continue a life of penance, lest he fail in the end.

As you begin crafting your spiritual warfare Battle Plan, take a moment to process the above verses, and where they may have convicted you regarding how seriously you avoid sin and seek grace.

1. In the sins that I know I repeat often, have I embraced a true and intense spirit of penance and dedication to removing that sin from my life? If not, what is holding me back?
2. Are there times when, after falling back into sin, I have seen that it has been more difficult to re-acquire the desire for prayer and holiness that I had before the fall?
3. Do I acknowledge that God is willing to bestow, and is actively offering, all the graces I need to become greater in holiness, or have I compromised with the world, and ceased desiring to make further progress in grace and virtue?

~PONDERANCE~

Man seeks happiness, but he cannot find that happiness apart from God. In order to secure man's eternal happiness, Our Lord became Incarnate and established His Church. He laid down His life on the Cross and, through His Death and Resurrection, won for us our redemption from sin and slavery to the devil.

When we enter into His Church, which is the New and Eternal Covenant, we die with Him, leave behind the old life that springs from Adam, and receive the grace of adoption as sons of God. This is done by the power of grace working through the Sacrament of Baptism. In this Sacrament, we die with Christ and rise again with Him as a new creation. The life of grace in our soul divinizes us[2] and configures us to the Image of the Second Person of the Blessed Trinity.

This glorious adoption is a gift from God to those who repent and cooperate with His activity in their soul. Here, sin becomes even more repulsive than it was when we were sinners separated from the Father. If we turn again to sin, like, as Proverbs says, the dog who returns to his vomit,[3] we willingly forfeit the promise of eternal glory and happiness with God in Heaven.

Thus, grace and sin are the two polar powers in the spiritual life. They cannot both abide in the soul. We must wholeheartedly leave behind the life of sin, and reject all forms of sin, even venial sin. Here, we must remember the distinction between mortal and venial sins. There are some sins which are mortal, deadly, and which kill the life of grace in the soul. There are others which are harmful, venial, but which only wound the connection and friendship we have with Christ.

If we persist in venial sin and do not seek to rid our lives of it, we will gradually grow weak and fall more easily into mortal sin. A life of cowardice in the face of temptation is one which will lead us to dislike the commands of Christ. Grace makes the yoke of Christ easy to bear, and the burden of His commands light. If we live without grace, we will grow bitter and resentful of the commands and example of Our Lord, by which we are instructed to adopt a penitential life, one which does not grow attached to the goods and pleasures of this world, but which tends to shun them for the sake of the Kingdom of Heaven.

Therefore, in life, our sins must be hated more than any other form of evil in the world. The fruit of our sins is misery in this life and damnation and eternal pain in the life to come.

Grace, contrarily, must be seen as the greatest good and the most powerful source of strength and happiness in this life, and the security for attaining the eternal life of glory after death.

---

[2] 2 Peter 1:4
[3] Proverbs 26:11

The Seriousness of Sin and Grace

A reminder of some essential points, from *Slaying Dragons*...

The Power of Grace
+ Christians are born for combat and, with the graces that Our Lord bestows on us through His Church, we have all the arms we need to do battle.
+ The more devout and holy we are, the more the devil fears us and is powerless against us.
+ The principal means of protection is to remain in a state of grace with a deep faith, which is nurtured and supported by frequent reception of Holy Communion and Confession.
+ A daily spiritual focus should include an emphasis on the virtue of humility and the need for prayer and meditation.

The Power and the Effects of Sin
+ When we sin, we essentially act like the demons and this opens doors to them.
+ Mortal sin cuts us off from God's grace and aligns us with the workings of Satan, making us vulnerable to diabolical influences, including possession.
+ These sins are referred to as gateway sins, which can open us individually to demons as well as make those in our family more vulnerable to their presence and influence.
+ All sins and vices damage us and create wounds, which are burdens that destabilize us and make us more vulnerable to diabolical influences.
+ The number of doorways to evil has greatly increased in modern times, and includes evils like pornography, that have become quite widespread.

Questions to consider:
- Have I come to view Christianity as a Sunday-only religion, in which I return to a rather secular life during the week, as if there were no real spiritual world, battle, or goals which hold importance in my life?
- When I am tempted to sin, in which I would fall out of a state of grace, do I first consider all that I would lose in the process?
- How often do I go to Confession? The Church recommends at least monthly Confession, since there are many benefits to the soul each time we receive this Sacrament, even if it were to be for venial sins only.
- Do I make light of sin, forgetting that each sin causes a wound, disrupts our relationship with God, and associates us, in some way, with the diabolical?
- In the times when I have avoided a sin or near occasion of sin, what helped me to do so?

_____

_____

_____

_____

Slaying Dragons – Prepare for Battle

The Seriousness of Sin and Grace

~CONSIDERATIONS~

#1. Demons operate with a "slow and steady" approach: they will chip away at our armor and our resolve until we consent to just the smallest sin. At that point, they apply more and more pressure against our desire for goodness. If we do not stop them early, they will win. What are the small sins in your life, which appear regularly, and which, upon reflection, you can see are connected to a cascade of other sins, including those that are mortal? Are you already taking these to Confession? What can you do to root out these sins?
- Small sins can dim our devotion. What habitual small sins are causing you to grow cold or uninterested in prayer and works of holiness?
- What are the small sins I should be taking to Confession more intently?
- Resolve to challenge these sins: laziness with renewed dedication, putting off prayer with getting up early to pray, impatience with prioritizing responsibilities, anger or pride with daily readings of the Gospels.
    - How can you immediately implement something new?
    - What do you foresee standing in your way as you seek to follow through with this implementation?
    - How would you overcome that obstacle?

_____
_____
_____
_____
_____
_____
_____
_____
_____

#2. The primary door to increased diabolical influence is a mortal sin. Mortal sins are nothing to take lightly; they kill the life of grace in the soul. Consider the mortal sins you struggle with.
- Are you sufficiently vigilant against them?
- Do you tolerate a mortal sin here or there, or give in to expressions of pride once in a while?
- What more, concretely, can you do to thwart your fall into mortal sin and your interest in those sins?
    - Perhaps a nightly examination of conscience, weekly Confession even for small (venial) compromises with that weakness, open up to a friend about your struggle, add a(nother) day of fasting in your week?

- Venial sins are essentially "gateways" to mortal sins, since they condition us to compromise on our fidelity to God's laws.
    - Do you regularly accuse yourself, and ask for forgiveness, for the small sins you commit throughout the day?
    - Do you have more concern for maintaining your earthly treasures and responsibilities than you do for your spiritual treasures and responsibilities?
    - If you are good at the management of earthly treasures, what can you take from that and apply to your spiritual management?
- In families, parishes, and religious communities, we are tasked with aiding each other to Heaven. When you notice someone's sin, do you desire, and seek, to help them correct their path, or do you rejoice that you are not as sinful as they are?

_____
_____
_____
_____
_____
_____
_____
_____
_____
_____
_____
_____
_____
_____
_____
_____

#3. When we reflect on the fact that demons are always observant of us, waiting for the moment when we align ourselves with them through grave sin, it should drive us to become rather militant about avoiding every sin, even venial sin!

The Seriousness of Sin and Grace

- How much do you fear sin, in the sense of its impact on your soul and its power to cause you to lose all good and holy things in your earthly and eternal life?
- Is this fear, while not scrupulous, sufficient to inspire you to complete the spiritual work which is necessary for you personally, that you may persevere and be saved?

_____
_____
_____
_____
_____
_____
_____
_____
_____

#4. Demons are, essentially, rather impulsive toward doing evil. This will animate them in Hell too, when they are in the company of the damned. Our own impulsivity toward evil could damn us as well. Reflect on how conditioned you are toward any specific vices and make a decision to nurture the virtue that most effectively counters it.

- Think about your daily routine. There are likely things you frequently do that you regret and which seem to happen without a deliberate choice on your part. Consider: are they emerging from anger, or fatigue, or control, or jealousy, or greed, or pride, etc.?
- List these specific sins and then try to understand which of the above (or other) vices might be prompting them.
- Then determine, with prayer and reflection, what is the best way to calm these vices before they manifest in sin, or to replace them with a virtuous manifestation in those same situations.

_____
_____
_____
_____
_____

#5. Am I prone to a quick temper or bursts of anger? Find a novena, such as one to Our Lady Undoer of Knots and plead with Our Lady to remove this vice from your life. If you don't notice the change you desired after the first 9 days, repeat the Novena. If you need some encouragement about being persistent in prayer, read Luke 11: 5-10 and Luke 18: 1-8.

#6. Reflect on the fact that, after Judgment, if you are not saved, you will **eternally** lose all the good things that you have accumulated in this life: God's gifts and the merits of your good deeds. All will be lost as a result of brief and fleeting moments of power or pleasure in this earthly life. Choose a small sacrifice to do daily or weekly that will serve as a reminder of your need for constant penance and detachment from earthly pleasures.
- What is a daily snack or sweet you enjoy? Give that up, for just a day (or more), and replace it with reading the Gospels for fifteen minutes.
- Is there a show you always watch, particularly if it doesn't have a helpful moral or religious influence on you? Skip that for one night (or more) and replace it with sitting in silence on the porch, reading the Gospels, calling your parents, or something you always neglect but which you know is good for you.

The Seriousness of Sin and Grace

#7. Take a moment and make a serious account of any mortal sins that you struggle with or for which you are tolerant. If you engage in gravely immoral practices, or encourage others in them, or give your support to them in society, you are opening a door for the diabolic to work in your life more easily and effectively.
- If you can identify any of these:
    - renounce them in the Name of Jesus,
    - use the binding prayer[4] against the specific demons that are tempting you in these areas,
    - and take these matters to Confession.

#8. Consider your habits of indulgence regarding a certain created thing, like a food or drink or style of leisure, a comfortable chair or a television show.
- How many times have you consciously over-indulged or becoming lazy in this activity?
- How many times has this notably made you less inclined toward prayer and less tolerant of the suffering that comes with pursuing a greater good?
- Once you can name this over-indulgence, do some concrete things to break this habit, such as
    - occasionally denying yourself that pleasure and going for a walk instead,
    - or checking one thing off of your to-do list.

---

[4] See *Binding Prayers* on page 183

#9. Have you ever justified any sins in part because they brought a sense of peace and "joy" into your life? What were those sins?
- Ponder your motivations for committing those acts.
    o What vices, forms of selfishness, or other motivations were present in your soul?
    o What benefit did you really gain from those sins?
    o In the end, did those sins lead to an easier life or to conflict, suffering, or increased hardship?

The Seriousness of Sin and Grace

#10. Make a list of the vices with which you primarily struggle. Do some research to see which Saints are the Patron Saints of those struggles. Study their lives and look for the examples and teachings that they provide that can help you break free of this habit. Invoke their assistance, especially when you use the binding prayer against this vice.

~ADDITIONAL NOTES FOR THIS SECTION~

The Seriousness of Sin and Grace

~PRAYER~

Take away, my God,
all that steals my heart from Thee.
Turn, O Lord,
my eyes toward eternal truths.
Give me, my Savior,
a distaste for the pleasures of this world.
Grant me true vision,
that I may see sin as horrific,
grace as most beautiful,
suffering as instructive
truth as nourishing,
and a life of holiness as the only way to true peace and happiness.
Amen.

III: Prayers and Devotions

Patron Saint: St. Margaret Mary Alacoque

~PRAYER~

To Thee, my God, I surrender,
and to Thy Saints I raise my voice
that they may hear from Heaven and take pity on me,
remembering the way which they too once walked
through this valley of tears and snares
where the Enemy prowls by night and by day.
O God, Thou art glorified in Thy Holy Angels and Saints!
May they, who proved themselves faithful to Thee,
dispense from the Heavenly altar
the goodness and protection Thou desirest to bestow upon us.
May they, who have conquered the dragon by the blood of the Lamb,
shield us with their prayers and fortify us with the graces they have won.
May their merits, together with those of our Queen,
liberate us from our bondage to sin and death, which we still suffer in this life.
Lifted up by this sacred communion,
may we come swiftly home to Thee, our Heavenly Father.
Amen.

~INTRODUCTION~

This life is a battlefield, onto which we were born and in which we were destined to engage in combat. This battlefield is the body, which wages war against the soul, and where many battle lines are drawn and our actions lead to the loss of grace or the acquisition of merit. Though this particular battle is within the individual man, he is not the only soldier fighting. The man is but one of many who are engaged in the battle over his soul: he fights, and Heaven fights with him, while Hell and its armies fight against him. Heaven and Hell are at war with each other over the formation and destiny of his soul.

This battle, though, can be easily won, if he completely aligns himself with God and the citizens of Heaven, in their efforts to incorporate him into their Kingdom. This work is known as prayer. It is in the intellect that Satan tempts him and it is in the intellect that, by prayer and meditation, his soul becomes docile and receptive to the superabundance of sanctifying grace. If a man masters the art and habit of prayer, he will be victorious in this fight over his immortal soul.

Reflections on Sacred Scripture
The following Scripture verses relate to the theme of this section. Read through them slowly, noticing what stands out in each passage. Does a verse convict you of something you are lacking? Does a verse confirm that you are being faithful, thus clearing away doubts? Does a verse strike your heart with a new understanding of God and His holy will?

~~~

~PSALM 5:1-3~
Give ear to my words, O LORD; give heed to my groaning. Hearken to the sound of my cry, my King and my God, for to thee do I pray. O LORD, in the morning thou dost hear my voice; in the morning I prepare a sacrifice for thee, and watch.

~PSALM 141:2~
Let my prayer be counted as incense before thee, and the lifting up of my hands as an evening sacrifice!

~PHILIPPIANS 4:6~
Have no anxiety about anything, but in everything by prayer and supplication with thanksgiving let your requests be made known to God.

~EPHESIANS 6:18~
Pray at all times in the Spirit, with all prayer and supplication. To that end keep alert with all perseverance, making supplication for all the saints.

~ROMANS 8:26~
Likewise the Spirit helps us in our weakness; for we do not know how to pray as we ought, but the Spirit himself intercedes for us with sighs too deep for words.

~JAMES 5: 16-18~
The prayer of a righteous man has great power in its effects. Elijah was a man of like nature with ourselves and he prayed fervently that it might not rain, and for three years and six months it did not rain on the earth. Then he prayed again and the heaven gave rain, and the earth brought forth its fruit.

~PSALM 66:18-19~
If I had cherished iniquity in my heart, the Lord would not have listened. But truly God has listened; he has given heed to the voice of my prayer.

~PROVERBS 15:29~
The LORD is far from the wicked, but he hears the prayer of the righteous.

Prayers and Devotions

~MATTHEW 7:11~
If you then, who are evil, know how to give good gifts to your children, how much more will your Father who is in heaven give good things to those who ask him!

~LUKE 18:6-8~
And the Lord [referring to His parable] said, "Hear what the unrighteous judge says. And will not God vindicate his elect, who cry to him day and night? Will he delay long over them? I tell you, he will vindicate them speedily.

~JOHN 15:7~
If you abide in me, and my words abide in you, ask whatever you will, and it shall be done for you.

~1 JOHN 5:14~
And this is the confidence which we have in him, that if we ask anything according to his will he hears us.

~LUKE 6:12~
In these days he went out into the hills to pray; and all night he continued in prayer to God.

From the Scriptures:
- We must look upon our prayers as a sacrifice that is pleasing to the Lord, and which He desires to receive from us.
- Before succumbing to fear or worry, we must present our prayers with confidence to our God.
- The Holy Spirit Himself will teach us how to pray, and will prompt us to pray well, that we may not give up nor become discouraged.
- The Lord responds quickly to the prayers of His faithful children, who excel in righteousness and humility, and who shun evil and repent.
- Our Lord instructs us to pray incessantly and He will hear and respond speedily.
- If we abide in Him, and are faithful and obedient to Him, whatever we ask, He will do.
- In imitation of Our Lord Jesus Christ, let us make sacrifices, even of sleep, in order to remain in prayer always.

As you begin crafting your spiritual warfare Battle Plan, take a moment to process the above verses, and where they may have convicted you regarding the confidence you place in the power of prayer.
1. Do I look upon prayer as a serious spiritual activity, with power, beauty, and efficacy, or as a burdensome requirement to satisfy God's demands?
2. When my prayer is difficult or dry, do I invoke the Holy Spirit to aid me and prompt me and pray within me?
3. Do I treasure being in the state of grace so the merit of my prayers may increase and I may become more capable of interceding for others?

Slaying Dragons – Prepare for Battle

Prayers and Devotions

~PONDERANCE~

Prayer is the mightiest work that man will do. In it, he resists the devil, the force of his fallen nature, and the chaos of the fallen world, and enters into the cave of simplicity and renunciation, in which he hears the quiet and calm voice of the Lord.

Prayer is the work of a hero, a mighty warrior, a victor on the spiritual battlefield. He is one who seeks the Captain of Souls, wisely looking past lesser forms of wisdom, the worldly counsels which instruct him to serve himself and his needs alone. Christ our Redeemer is our Deliverer from evil and its many consequences, including that internal weakness which threatens our eternal happiness.

It is in and through prayer that He calls each one of us onto the battlefield, where we face both the "principalities, the powers, the world rulers of this present darkness, the spiritual hosts of wickedness in the heavenly places"[1] – and ourselves. The world has been formed by the influence of the Evil One, and we too have become compromised to the extent that we have accepted his invitations to prefer our own designs and desires over the will and commands and love of God.

Prayer joins us to the Bridegroom and to the Bride, to God and to His Church, to supernatural charity and to those holy ones who live within it. The presence of the Holy Spirit in the soul who prays changes the way the person lives and breathes and moves. This change has already been completed in the Angels and the Saints who have been eternally united to the Most Blessed Trinity. Thus, through prayer, we enjoy the fruit of adoption into the family of God: countless older brothers and sisters whose moral and spiritual excellence is far superior to anything we have ever encountered on this earth.

When we pray to the Angels and the Saints, it is not because we have no hope that Our Lord will hear us, and that they are our last recourse to obtain aid as we walk through this valley of tears. No, they are our friends, our fellow warriors, our leaders and the commanders of the battalions of the Lord. God Himself has placed them among us in order to hand on His orders, His grace, and His weapons, that mankind may be saved by Him through His Church, through the cooperation of the citizens of the Kingdom of Heaven.

Man is not left alone in this life; not by God, nor by those who love Him. While we await entrance into eternal glory, where we will behold Him face-to-face and hear His voice, we are led there by His ministers, who instruct us by their example and aid us by their intercession, pulling us by their strength along the way, when we are too weak to progress on our own.

Bring the Angels and the Saints, and above all the Holy Mother of God, into your daily journey, that they may teach you how to love God well and may encourage you with foretastes of the eternal delights which they already behold.

---

[1] Cf. Eph 6:12

Slaying Dragons – Prepare for Battle

A reminder of some essential points, from *Slaying Dragons*...

+ The angels and the saints constantly work against the actions of the demons. Certain saints are pitted against certain demons to specifically block and oppose their evil efforts.
+ The work of the Communion of Saints is essential; exorcists see how much the demons hate us and them, often from the mouths of the demons themselves.
+ A devotion to Our Lady is one of the most powerful means to obtain an abundance of grace from Our Lord and protection against the workings of the Evil One.
+ Many people in the Church today are afraid, ignorant, or unbelieving regarding the existence of Satan and the necessity of exorcisms.
+ St. Alphonsus says, "Meditation is the blessed furnace in which divine love is lighted up."[2]

Questions to consider:
- Is there a Saint who endured certain evils or sufferings in his life which are similar to the ones that burden you the most? Research about that Saint and find a prayer to him to recite on a daily basis, or a novena.
- Do you read the lives of the Saints often? They are filled with the true accounts of how God works steadily in the souls of those who simply stay close to Him.
- When you meditate on God's revelation, do you reflect on the power which it has to move your soul away from sin and toward holiness? Even though you are frail and weak, meditation obtains powerful spiritual effects which bring true supernatural strength.

___

[2] *Preparation for Death,* p 323. St. Alphonsus equates mental prayer with meditation.

Prayers and Devotions

~CONSIDERATIONS~

#1. Thoughts, burdened by what may be diabolical obsession, can be liberated by meditation, such as by praying the Holy Rosary. The Rosary can be aided with the use of the Gospels. There are "scriptural Rosary" guides easily available online or through bookstores. The Gospels themselves can also be used to aid meditation. *Lectio divina* is a traditional way of reading the Gospels and praying in order to meditate. An easy guide to *lectio divina* can also be found online.
- If you already knew this power of meditation, how often do you set aside a focused time to engage in meditation?
- Or, if you just learned it, how willing are you to take up this powerful means of meditation on a daily basis?[3]
- Are there certain mysteries of the Rosary, like the Crowning with Thorns, or sections in the Gospels, like the Agony in the Garden, that really capture your mind in meditation and make it easy to engage in mental prayer? Note these and return to these as often as you need to.
- Do you know how to pray, or how to find time for prayer? A good guide is a book I wrote called, *Come Away By Yourselves*, which lays out a practical approach to prayer for busy Catholics.

_____
_____
_____
_____
_____
_____
_____

#2. Exorcists learn a lot about their ministry, especially in the beginning of their work, by simply watching an exorcism. The more they carry out the Rite themselves, the wiser they become. Prayer and the spiritual life are very similar for us. The more we pray thoughtfully and attentively, and the more we listen to the voice of God in prayer, the more we understand the art of prayer.
- Consider keeping a prayer journal to write down your prayers and chronicle what you perceive God is saying to you. Over time, these notes will help you see how God has been prompting you and acting in your life.
- Remember, prayer is similar to other human habits: if we stop practicing the art, we will grow cold and forgetful. The art of prayer and listening to God must be kept up daily or we will spend far too much time re-learning to pray that much potential for progress will be lost.

---

[3] Meditation is also called mental prayer. It is where we, in God's presence, reflect on Him and on things related to Him, such as the mysteries of faith and God's will for us.

- Make a list of the different forms of prayer that you engage in on the average week (Rosary, Scripture, Mass readings, Missal readings, Litanies, morning offering, examination, etc.): how well are you maintaining your "prayer strength"? Is there one on this list that you would like to add to your routine? What would it take to make this happen?

_____

_____

_____

_____

_____

_____

_____

#3. The Holy Name of Jesus is very powerful in the spiritual life. Consider finding an engraving or a painting of the Holy Name and place it in a prominent place in your home. When you look at it, pronounce His Holy Name with confidence, renewing your fidelity to Him and requesting His blessing and protection. If you are even slightly artistic, consider making one yourself. This personal investment into glorifying the Holy Name will be of great benefit to your soul. If you have children, be sure to teach them the importance of the Holy Name of Jesus as well.

#4. Consecrating yourself and all of your possessions to the Mother of God is a powerful means of placing these things out of reach of the diabolical. A prayer was composed by a few exorcists for this purpose and is listed in Part II.[4]

#5. When I pray, does it reflect the reality that I am in a war against a highly organized diabolical system? Is my prayer a bit "soft" or lackadaisical in the absence of serious reflection on the truth and gravity of this spiritual battle?
- Set aside some time today to develop a real game plan:
    o What steps can I take to increase my prayer life?
    o What times in the day are ideal for me to pray?
    o What sort of good deeds am I lacking in and could easily bring into my daily routine?
    o What are the aspects of the Catholic Faith for which I do not have a sufficient understanding and knowledge?
- Consider establishing a specific and comfortable spot in your house where you can easily pray. Make it appealing, either simple or adorned with sacred images and a candle, etc.

---

[4] Called "Consecration of One's Exterior Goods to the Blessed Virgin Mary" on page 185

Prayers and Devotions

_____
_____
_____
_____
_____
_____
_____
_____
_____
_____

#6. The Church's tradition and the experience of the faithful have given countless examples of the reality of Purgatory and the experience of souls who dwell there.
- Make a list of all your deceased family members and friends and schedule a Mass to be said for each of them. The parish secretary will be able to arrange the dates. Try to have the Mass offered on the anniversary of their deaths. It is highly likely, at a bigger parish, that the Masses will be scheduled for the following year, due to the number of people requesting Masses for various reasons.
    - o Make use of the feast days of the Church, esp. November 2nd and the month of November. Visit a cemetery to pray for the souls of the faithful departed. If you have children, take them along with you. There is a specific indulgence attached to praying for the souls in Purgatory between November 1st and 8th.[5]
    - o You can offer your rosaries and indulgences for them.
    - o Collect the names of the deceased here to get started:

_____
_____
_____
_____
_____

---

[5] Indulgences, through the intercession of the Church, assist souls by removing part or all of the temporal punishment due to sins already forgiven, thus especially aiding those who are in Purgatory awaiting the completion of the purification of their souls, that they may then enter Heaven and finally see God face-to-face.

_____

_____

_____

_____

_____

_____

#7. The Saints in Heaven are with us in this war against the diabolical. Remember to invoke them daily. The Saints you are inclined to may actually be the very ones you need by your side in battle. Make a list of the Saints you love the most and determine the best time each day to invoke their assistance.

_____

_____

_____

_____

_____

_____

_____

_____

#8. Work on building your friendship with God. Talk to Him about your day, your life, your blessings, your struggles, etc. You may be surprised by the transformation it brings about, and who else may be inspired to imitate you in order to have the joy that you possess.

#9. Pray for all of your family members. Have Masses offered for them and make personal sacrifices for them. If you have children, pray for your children often. Consider dedicating a certain time (like a week or a month) and pray for your children on each day with a certain intention such as "that they may grow in love of Jesus."
- Make regular visits to a Church or Chapel to pray. Take friends or family along with you if possible.
- When you agree to pray for someone, fulfill that promise immediately so you do not forget and so you nurture a stronger spirit of prayer.

Prayers and Devotions

~ADDITIONAL NOTES FOR THIS SECTION~

Slaying Dragons – Prepare for Battle

~Prayer~

My God,
Thy voice is subtle, but a whisper to my soul.
I often cannot hear it for the distractions in my life.
Captivate me and set my mind upon heavenly things,
that thereupon I may take notice of Thy beauty and goodness.
Draw me after Thee, O Lord.
Set a fire of truth in my mind, that my thoughts may be purified and desire only Thee.
Craft, O Lord, a furnace of meditation in my soul,
where the glory of Thy revelation may be enshrined.
Assign to me Thy holy friends, the many Angels and Saints,
that they may teach me and encourage me to follow after Thee in all my thoughts.
Without Thy grace, I will turn away to earthly cares and passions.
Crucify my flesh that I may no longer be a man of this world but a man of heaven.
Amen.

IV: General Spiritual Warfare

Patron Saint: St. Joseph

~PRAYER~

Most powerful Savior,
I entrust my life, from my earliest days to this present moment,
to Thy mercy and love.
Many times, I have strayed from the way Thou hast set before me,
meriting Thy just displeasure and the disordering of my soul.
Cleanse me, O Lord, by the graces that flow from Thy Sacred Wounds,
and which are poured out upon me through Thy Holy Church.
Sanctify me and separate me from the evils I have formerly embraced.
Stir up a holy zeal in me now, that I may, with the full force of my will,
renounce my lingering attachments to the sins I have committed.
Forgive me for the many times I have offended Thee.
Heal the wounds in my soul,
and drive afar the agents of evil and death who prowl within my life, seeking my destruction.
Place the sword of Thy Spirit in my hands and send me out into battle that,
remaining always beneath Thy standard,
I may triumph over my enemies and secure the crown of salvation Thou holdest out before me.
Amen.

~INTRODUCTION~

Spiritual warfare involves a man's entire life. From waking to sleeping, he must be on guard against temptations and weaknesses, snares and memories, desires and emotions. Most of the time, this warfare is subtle and simple, involving custody of the mind and prudent living, in addition to the standard life of prayer and the Sacraments.

However, there is never a moment when man is able to rest while he continues his pilgrimage on the way to eternal life. Thus, even a man who is strong in faith, immersed in grace, and consistent in prayer, needs to keep vigil against the craftiness of the Enemy. Even this man can daily make more and more progress in the spiritual life, and more securely establish the hope of his salvation.

Reflections on Sacred Scripture
The following Scripture verses relate to the theme of this section. Read through them slowly, noticing what stands out in each passage. Does a verse convict you of something you are lacking? Does a verse confirm that you are being faithful, thus clearing away doubts? Does a verse strike your heart with a new understanding of God and His holy will?

~~~

~PSALM 23: 4-6~
Even though I walk through the valley of the shadow of death, I fear no evil; for thou art with me; thy rod and thy staff, they comfort me. Thou preparest a table before me in the presence of my enemies; thou anointest my head with oil, my cup overflows. Surely goodness and mercy shall follow me all the days of my life; and I shall dwell in the house of the LORD for ever.

~2 KINGS 6:16-17~
He said, "Fear not, for those who are with us are more than those who are with them." Then Elisha prayed, and said, "O LORD, I pray thee, open his eyes that he may see." So the LORD opened the eyes of the young man, and he saw; and behold, the mountain was full of horses and chariots of fire round about Elisha.

~EXODUS 15:3 DR~
The Lord is a man of war, Almighty is his name.

~ROMANS 16:20~
And the God of peace crush Satan under your feet speedily.

~2 CORINTHIANS 12:7-9~
And to keep me from being too elated by the abundance of revelations, a thorn was given me in the flesh, a messenger of Satan, to harass me, to keep me from being too elated. Three times I besought the Lord about this, that it should leave me; [but] he said to me, "My grace is sufficient for you, for my power is made perfect in weakness." I will all the more gladly boast of my weaknesses, that the power of Christ may rest upon me.

~EPHESIANS 6:12~
For we are not contending against flesh and blood, but against the principalities, against the powers, against the world rulers of this present darkness, against the spiritual hosts of wickedness in the heavenly places.

~JAMES 4:7~
Submit yourselves therefore to God. Resist the devil and he will flee from you.

~1 JOHN 3:8~
The reason the Son of God appeared was to destroy the works of the devil.

General Spiritual Warfare

~DEUTERONOMY 3:22~
You shall not fear them; for it is the LORD your God who fights for you.

~COLOSSIANS 2:15~
He disarmed the principalities and powers and made a public example of them, triumphing over them in him.

~JOHN 10:10~
The thief comes only to steal and kill and destroy; I came that they may have life, and have it abundantly.

~1 JOHN 4:4 DR~
You are of God, little children, and have overcome him. Because greater is he that is in you, than he that is in the world.

From the Scriptures:
- With the Lord at our side, we can live in the midst of death and enemies and still have no fear in our hearts nor fail in our strength.
- Our Lord has stationed a mighty army among us, ready to come to our aid, hidden but speedily deployed, through which He will crush the demons and establish us in peace.
- God will not let us find strength only in our own power and nature, for we must rely on his grace more if we are to stand against the great fallen spiritual powers that have set themselves against us.
- If we are docile to His Spirit and humbly obedient to His commands, the devil will flee from us as from one like the Son of God Himself.
- If we allow Christ's life to flow abundantly within us, we shall overcome the Enemy by the power of God, who has disarmed them by the power of His Cross.

As you begin crafting your spiritual warfare Battle Plan, take a moment to process the above verses, and where they may have convicted you regarding your confidence in Our Lord's protection.
1. Do I see that all my trials and troubles are nothing to fear, and not powerful enough to crush me, if I cling to God and walk trustingly beside His love and power?
2. Do I tremble as the world crumbles more and more beneath evil, forgetful that Our Lord has not revoked the mighty army of angels who are positioned to defend, comfort, and protect us?
3. Have I noticed how, in times of devotion and trust, I am generally more content with life, and in times where prayer wains, I am more inclined to fear, control, and anxiety?

_____

_____

_____

_____

Slaying Dragons – Prepare for Battle

General Spiritual Warfare

~PONDERANCE~

Christians are born for combat. The perennial wisdom of the Church, and that of Christ and the Apostles themselves, is that we are in a state of perpetual warfare in this world. The whole world is in a state of warfare, but Christians actually wield weapons in the battle.

When we were in darkness, we wandered in the world with open and empty hands, powerless against our enemies and ready to be led by them. We were blind men wandering after the voices of other blind men speaking in the darkness of the world. We knew not the path to take nor where the paths we took would lead us. Utterly without wisdom or direction, we served the gods of this world, the fallen spirits who demand we obey them and imitate their rebellion in the absence of Christ's illumination.

Thus, rescued through Baptism from the path of destruction, the way that leads to the pit, which the world cultivates and celebrates, we now find ourselves standing against the evil ones who thought the whole world had fallen into their hands. If this were the final description, we would never stand a chance of victory, but through us, in us, before us, behind us, beside us, above us, and below us, Christ the conqueror of sin and death reigns in His glory – and the demons know it.

His solemn and soothing voice commands us to courage and to take up the weapons that lay at our feet, which He placed there beside the waters of regeneration. Armed, we now wage war with the fortitude of the Holy Spirit, against the principalities, against the powers, against the world rulers of this present darkness, against the spiritual hosts of wickedness in the heavenly places – and we do so without fear.

When we stand with Christ in our eyes, His victory in our mind, His love in our hearts, and His gifts adorning us, there is no worse terror for a demon to behold. Armed with prayer, the Sacraments, the sacramentals, the Communion of Saints, and the merits of holiness, the demons will be crushed in the stampede of their retreat.

St. Jean Vianney encourages us in this warfare, stating:

> "We can do nothing by ourselves, my children; but we can do everything with the help of the good God; let us pray Him to deliver us from this enemy of our salvation, or to give us strength to fight against him. With the Name of Jesus we shall overthrow the demons; we shall put them to flight. With this Name, if they sometimes dare to attack us, our battles will be victories, and our victories will be crowns for Heaven, all brilliant with precious stones."[1]

Take courage and take arms, for the war is underway and the spoils of victory is to the one who conquers!

---

[1] St. Jean Vianney, *Little Catechism of the Cure of Ars*, TAN books, 1994, p. 99

A reminder of some essential points on spiritual warfare from *Slaying Dragons*…

+ The diabolical attack on mankind began with Eve – and pride is at the root of all of their sins.
+ We must learn how to fight well and perseveringly against the demons.
+ Humility, mental prayer and meditation, and recourse to our Guardian Angels are means to protect us against diabolical obsession.
+ For those liberated from possession, it is critical that the person protect his spiritual life so as not to relapse into sin and suffer a worse re-possession.
+ Exorcisms, binding prayers, and deliverance prayers are all part of the rich heritage of the Catholic Faith, though few people today are properly aware of them.
+ The binding prayer is an essential tool that all the faithful can use to protect themselves against the ordinary attacks of the Enemy.[2]
+ One of the powers and purposes of Baptism is to break and remove the presence of any demons in the child.
+ Invoking the aid of the Blessed Virgin Mary under the title "Our Lady of Sorrows" is particularly helpful in detecting and removing demons from our lives.[3]
+ Faith and a serious focus on God are sufficient to protect us against possession and serious diabolical influence.
+ Catholics should nurture a devout and frequent use of the sacramentals of the Church, such as approved medals, statues, scapulars, holy water, holy oil, blessed salt, blessed candles, sacred images, and sacred relics.
+ Fasting will increase how repugnant we are to the demons and help to drive them away, with the help of a prudent and frequent use of binding prayers.
+ It is important to know the history of your family, your neighborhood, your home, and areas you frequent to ensure that no diabolical doorways have been opened by means of these.

Questions to consider:
- Do you take time each day to evaluate the spiritual warfare you are engaged in, such as the number of temptations you are involved in, including the subtle temptations from the world as presented in the culture?
- Is your devotional life rich with a variety of resources, such as novenas, chaplets, and the many sacramentals that are intended to fill the lives of Christians?[4]
- What more could you prudently add to your spiritual routine of prayer, such that you are not overwhelmed but are more thoroughly enriched?

---

[2] See *Binding Prayers* on page 183
[3] See page 199 and 203 for prayers and meditations related to Our Lady of Sorrows.
[4] See Part II for some of these prayers, novenas, Chaplets, etc.

General Spiritual Warfare

Slaying Dragons – Prepare for Battle

~CONSIDERATIONS~

#1. Looking at your family dynamics, are there any sins or vices or bad habits across multiple generations that are obvious, or that are detectable upon reflection? If so, and if they are of concern, do some thinking, and even some research on your family history, and see if you can uncover the root of those influences. This reflection will likely uncover particular weaknesses which have not only affected your family line but are also affecting you.

_____

_____

_____

_____

_____

_____

_____

#2. If you have been burdened with an addiction or a depression that hangs around, particularly one that is intense or does not seem to improve, consider meeting with a priest to get his perspective and counsel on the situation. If he thinks a deliverance prayer, or a minor exorcism prayer, might be helpful, he can do that while you are with him.[5]
- Depression and addiction can develop for a variety of reasons. However, the devil can cling to those wounds and make things worse.
- Remember, Our Lord healed people of both illnesses <u>and</u> diabolical influence. As a result, the prayers of His priests can bring real healing and comfort.
- If you suffer from depression, make a note of the things that occupy your mind when you feel this way:
    o Are these thoughts true, lies, or twisted truths?
    o Is Our Lord capable of addressing and healing these wounds and fears? (Of course, the answer is yes, but reflect on the fact that He can and desires to.)

_____

_____

_____

_____

_____

_____

---
[5] In addition to seeing a Catholic counselor, if need be.

#3. As crazy as it may sound, some people do enter into pacts with the devil or with a specific demon. This can occur in adulthood but also during periods of youthful curiosity or confusion. Think back and make sure that, if you had wild days in your youth, you are aware of whether you ventured into something like this.
- We often make friends with people whose personalities draw us to participate in their wild ideas. Do you recall any?
- If you are aware of any participation in something that resembled a pact with a demon, be sure to speak to a good priest about it soon.[6]

_____

_____

_____

_____

_____

#4. For those in married life: Consider the quality of openness and communication between you and your spouse. Sometimes, married life gets so busy that there is no time set aside for real conversation about what is pressing on the minds and hearts of the spouses. This communication is invaluable as it can prevent the diabolical from interfering with the unity in the home.
- Do you share the things that truly matter, such as any struggles with serious sin, any feelings of hurt or offense from the other spouse?
- Do you feel like there is an obstacle that prevents you from speaking to your spouse about the most important things? Perhaps a lack of trust, or a fear of rejection, or a fear of criticism, or a fear of looking weak or sinful in their eyes?
- Analyze this situation, name any hindrances, see if they are related to any sins, take anything to Confession that you need to, and then entrust these specific concerns to Our Lady, Undoer of Knots.[7]

If you are not married, read through the questions and see if there are any hindrances that prevent you from opening up to family, friends, God, new relations, vocational paths, etc.

_____

_____

_____

---

[6] See page 177 for *An Interior Healing Process*
[7] Pg. 195

#5. The Rite of Exorcism inflicts a real pain and suffering upon the demons who are possessing a person. Sacramentals work in a similar way and are used as part of the Rite. These sacred signs and vessels truly make you and your home less desirable and approachable to the demons. They would suffer much more to enter your home if it were well fortified with God's blessings.
- Have you fortified your home with sacramentals yet?
- Make a list of the sacramentals that you still need in your home and what you plan to do with them.
- Holy water bottle in most rooms? Crucifix in every room? Sacred images, blessed salt on the table or elsewhere, blessed medals placed strategically, etc.
- Then, invite the priest over for a meal, to bless the house (if not already done), and to give the traditional Roman Ritual blessing to each item.
- Learn well the wording of these blessings so you can fully appreciate them and use them devoutly as a gift from God.
- If you have children, teach the children about the sacramentals and what the blessings say.
- Embrace the full liturgical year and all of the sacramentals from the traditional Roman Ritual that are blessed on specific days, like candles on Candlemas, Epiphany water on Epiphany, blessed wine on St. John the Evangelist. If your priest does not currently offer these, inquire with him if he could begin to do so.

#6. Do you constantly look back at a sin you committed in the past? If there is still a lingering wound from this sin, establish a plan to attain true healing.
- Do you feel a certain negative power from the wound that it caused in your soul?
- Have you confessed this sin to a priest?
- Confess it again, and any current sins that seem to be related to it.
- Do a novena to Our Lady of Sorrows and Our Lady, Undoer of Knots with the intention of being healed completely of this wound; and go to Confession and to Mass at the end of the Novena and ask Our Lord to grant you the grace of liberation from this wound and all of its effects. (Pick a date for the Novena and Mass)

Slaying Dragons – Prepare for Battle

General Spiritual Warfare
~ADDITIONAL NOTES FOR THIS SECTION~

Slaying Dragons – Prepare for Battle

~PRAYER~

Grant, O Lord, I beseech Thee,
the grace to know the greatness of Thy Holy Name.
Indelibly sealed within my soul in Baptism, the mark of Thy Holy Name gives me courage.
Clinging to Thee,
and filled with gratitude for Thy Most Precious Blood, which has conquered all evils in this world,
I can stand tall in the midst of the perpetual warfare waged against Thy disciples.
Let me see the true nature of this battle and the many wiles and hooks and darts of the enemy
which have stung me and which must be removed and healed.
I accept, and I believe, O Lord,
that Thou hast truly given us all the power and grace we need
to be holy, powerful, and victorious.
Triumph in me, O Lord.
Triumph over evil in me, and triumph over evil through me.
Let me never be separated from Thee but make me secure in Thy grace.
Amen.

V: Being Strategic in Spiritual Warfare

Patron Saint: St. Ignatius of Loyola

~PRAYER~

Pour forth Thy wisdom, O Eternal God,
that, seeing the battle which rages for my soul,
I may not cower before my enemy,
nor protest the injustice of my plight,
but with the strength of Our Lord Jesus Christ
valiantly take up arms to engage it.
Fortify me with knowledge,
and with fortitude steel my nerves
that, abiding in Thy grace,
I may route this infernal foe and cut him down
when he manifests his malicious designs in my life.
Lead me through these tainted valleys
and aid me as I plot my course.
Send forth Thy mighty Spirit and,
through Thy angels and Thy saints,
bring divine light and liberty to my paths.
Amen.

~INTRODUCTION~

The man who stored up for himself earthly treasures, sufficient to provide for his needs for years to come, laid down to rest and, in his leisure and abundance, forsook the Lord and the demands of the spiritual life. He had become his own master and had seen to his own needs, and thus he enjoyed the fruits of his labor here and enjoyed the kingdom he had carved out for himself.[1]

The Enemy, who works well in the shadows, had first sown in the man's heart anxieties about life, and later the belief that he had done enough and was deserving of rest. The Enemy lured him into a rest that was a servitude to the flesh but an imprisonment of the spirit.

There, in that rest, we see an inverse of Jael's victory over Sisera.[2] She, the great victor over the Captain of Israel's enemy, lured him into a rest and into an unforeseen death. Likewise does the devil sneak into our tent, when we imprudently rest from battle, and devour our souls.

---

[1] Luke 12:20
[2] Judges 4:21

Reflections on Sacred Scripture

The following Scripture verses relate to the theme of this section. Read through them slowly, noticing what stands out in each passage. Does a verse convict you of something you are lacking? Does a verse confirm that you are being faithful, thus clearing away doubts? Does a verse strike your heart with a new understanding of God and His holy will?

~~~

~EPHESIANS 6:10-11, 14-17~
Finally, be strong in the Lord and in the strength of his might. Put on the whole armor of God, that you may be able to stand against the wiles of the devil. Stand therefore, having girded your loins with truth, and having put on the breastplate of righteousness, and having shod your feet with the equipment of the gospel of peace; ^{above} all taking the shield of faith, with which you can quench all the flaming darts of the evil one. And take the helmet of salvation, and the sword of the Spirit, which is the word of God.

~HEBREWS 12: 1-2~
Therefore, since we are surrounded by so great a cloud of witnesses, let us also lay aside every weight, and sin which clings so closely, and let us run with perseverance the race that is set before us, looking to Jesus the pioneer and perfecter of our faith, who for the joy that was set before him endured the cross, despising the shame, and is seated at the right hand of the throne of God.

~JOSHUA 1:9~
Have I not commanded you? Be strong and of good courage; be not frightened, neither be dismayed; for the LORD your God is with you wherever you go.

~DEUTERONOMY 28:7~
The LORD will cause your enemies who rise against you to be defeated before you; they shall come out against you one way, and flee before you seven ways.

~ISAIAH 54:17~
No weapon that is fashioned against you shall prosper, and you shall confute every tongue that rises against you in judgment. This is the heritage of the servants of the LORD and their vindication from me, says the LORD.

~2 CORINTHIANS 10:3-5~
For though we live in the world we are not carrying on a worldly war, for the weapons of our warfare are not worldly but have divine power to destroy strongholds. We destroy arguments and every proud obstacle to the knowledge of God, and take every thought captive to obey Christ.

~1 PETER 5:8-9~
Be sober, be watchful. Your adversary the devil prowls around like a roaring lion, seeking some one to devour. Resist him, firm in your faith.

Being Strategic in Spiritual Warfare

~2 THESSALONIANS 3:3~
The Lord is faithful; he will strengthen you and guard you from evil

~ROMANS 8:37~
In all these things we are more than conquerors through him who loved us.

From the Scriptures:
- Our Lord has revealed to us the Battle Plan we must adopt, against which the Enemy will have no recourse, and will flee: truth, righteousness, peace, faith, grace, and the Holy Spirit.
- We must do what is necessary to win the race of faith, modeling our course after that run by Jesus Christ Himself, persevering to the end in pursuit of the joy of God's eternal presence.
- Our Lord has directly told us to be not afraid, for the enemies that come against us will be destroyed by His own power, and every weapon of the Enemy will be thwarted by His love.
- The weapons Christ has given us have divine power and are effective in cutting down the lies and wiles of the Devil.
- Through Our Lord, who will never leave us, we will have the strength and protection to obtain the victory in this fight for our redemption.

As you begin crafting your spiritual warfare Battle Plan, take a moment to process the above verses, and where they may have convicted you regarding how well you follow the counsels of Our Lord.
1. In everything you do, does your heart have the certainty and confidence that God is active and ready to apply His divine power to the obstacles in your life?
2. How much of the burden of life's problems comes from fear and a lack of faith in God's promise to protect you and lead you through adversity and trial?
3. Have you reflected sufficiently on the promise that the weapons of spiritual warfare possess a "divine power"?

_____
_____
_____
_____
_____
_____
_____

Slaying Dragons – Prepare for Battle

Being Strategic in Spiritual Warfare

~PONDERANCE~

Many people wander through this life wondering what is the point, or meaning, of everything we see and experience: the meaning of life. Sadly, in this present age in particular, many Catholics also wander through life asking the same question. This philosophical question is good, but not when it reveals that the individual does not know the answer.

Catholics do know the answer to the question of the meaning of life. We are here to know, love, and serve God, that we may one day, by persevering in grace, come to live with Him forever in Heaven. The intensity of distractions and distractedness with which we all must suffer in this life leads far too many to set aside this knowledge.

When this happens, it is not just the knowledge of religion which begins to grow cold, but the desire to act in accordance with that knowledge. Those who lay aside the knowledge of the holy Catholic Faith also lay down the weapons placed in their hands by Almighty God. The same God who revealed the Truth revealed that we are in the midst of a devastating and brutal war, initiated by invisible enemies whose subtleties and craftiness are their main weapons. When we stop listening to God's Revelation, becoming forgetful of it, we stop planning our lives around it.

If we do not make a plan for engagement in this war, but act as if the war did not exist, we fool ourselves and fall into the easiest traps of the Enemy. If we think he is not there, then we will never resist his voice, which will continue to bombard our minds regardless of whether we acknowledge it. In that state, we will slowly be molded into the image of the Enemy himself and grow to loathe and despise our Creator as he does.

This plan must include recourse to the means of acquiring grace: prayer, devotion, Sacraments, sacramentals, Sacred Scripture, and the wisdom of the Saints. Among these latter, hear the counsel of St. Jean Vianney, on acquiring the grace to love God and despise evil:

> "So if you were to keep Our Lord well and recollectedly, after Communion, you would long feel the devouring fire which would inspire your heart with an inclination to good and a repugnance to evil. When we have the good God in our heart, it ought to be very burning. The heart of the disciples of Emmaus burnt within them from merely listening to His voice."[3]

In this life, we have all the supernatural resources we need to engage this war properly. We must take them up! In this life, there is no time to rest from the warfare.

We must not build little kingdoms for ourselves, kingdoms of dirt, but make ourselves into mighty Temples of the Holy Spirit, whose towers are in the heavens.

---

[3] *The Little Catechism of the Cure of Ars*, p 44-45

Slaying Dragons – Prepare for Battle

A reminder of some essential points, from *Slaying Dragons*...

+ Demons are real, personal, rational, spiritual beings who chose evil and set themselves in opposition to God and man.
+ Demons are fallen angels. They possess the same kind of nature as the holy angels, but with limitations.
+ Demons drive us to extremes and do everything they can to prevent us from thinking about God.
+ Demons prefer to work in hidden ways but will work extraordinarily to make us suffer more. When they manifest, it damages their plan, because it brings their existence into the light.
+ Demons are permitted to influence our minds and our bodies and our external lives. Some of these influences are common, some are rare.
+ Exorcists have learned how demons think and how they are motivated by different sins as well as the psychology which they each have as individual spirits.
+ Demons seek to divide and attack and frustrate us.
+ Angels merited beatification at the first moment after they were created, when they chose to obey God's will and serve Him. This is the same moment when the demons chose to disobey.
+ Demons know that what they lost in Heaven we will one day gain by grace.
+ The angelic intellect is very keen and perceptive of all things and is given immense infused knowledge by God.
+ Though they cannot see the future, their vast knowledge and intellectual powers gives them an impressive ability to perceive and predict the course that the future will take. Neither the angels nor the demons can actually see the future.
+ Once the angels made their choice, their wills became fixed in this decision, because they had perfect clarity regarding their choice.
+ There are demons that specifically target the family, so it is important that the father, and the whole family, stay devoted to Our Lord and in a state of grace.
+ Authority also exists within the family structure. The father of the family may bless all the members of the family. The father and mother may do binding prayers over each other and their children.
+ Demons know who has authority and who does not. Only those with proper authority should proceed with an exorcism or use the name of a demon.
+ Those without the authority of the Church often cause more problems than solutions in their attempt to cast out demons.

Questions to consider:
- The devil seduced Adam and Eve, to whose weakness we are bound through our nature – do you seek to shed the old man with his deeds,[4] whom Satan knows he can win over?
- The Saints were more than victorious over the Enemy – do you seek to study their ways and imitate their virtues, penances, and prayers, in order to share in their victory?

---
[4] Col 3:9

Being Strategic in Spiritual Warfare

~CONSIDERATIONS~

#1. The father of the family occupies a vital role of both spiritual and temporal authority which must be fulfilled. This role can be a source of grace for all in the home, or an obstacle to spiritual growth.
- In your current family, and in your family when you were young, was there a laxity or a disregard for the paternal authority in the home?
- Was there a spiritual weakness in the father in the home?
- What impact, positive or negative, did you, or do you now, see from the kind of role that the father in the family has played in your own life?
- Be sure to say a prayer for your father and entrust him to St. Joseph.
- If you are a father, do you seek guidance from Our Lord in all your ways? How healthy is your spiritual life? Children are very perceptive: are your children observing and imitating your sincere love for Our Lord?

_____
_____
_____
_____
_____
_____
_____
_____
_____
_____

#2. Fathers, you can daily bless your wife and children. Parents, you can daily pray for your children, offer a sacrifice to atone for their sins, and pray the binding prayers for them as needed. Set aside some time to seriously consider the needs of your children and any struggles that could use your authoritative prayers. Reflect on the sins you know they struggle with and ask the Holy Spirit to teach you how to guide them accordingly.
- If you are married, are you observing the proper authority structure in your family?
- When are ideal times for you to bless you children (morning, bedtime, before school) and for you to pray for their spiritual protection and strength?
- When are ideal times or days of the week to sit and talk with your children to learn more about their thoughts, needs, struggles, etc.?

#3. If you are married, are you praying for your spouse? Are you making sure that you spend quality time together in order to nurture the love that models Christ and His Church?
- Do you continue to have "date nights?"
- Does your spouse feel your love in your words and deeds: your time, prayers, service, touch, sacrifices, etc.?
- If you are separated from your spouse, are you still praying for your spouse and offering sacrifices on their behalf?

#4. Knowing that Satan and the demons are carrying out an organized and strategic attack on you personally, how might you craft an organized and strategic spiritual defense system and counterattack?
- Make a list of the places of weakness in your life:
  o habitual sins, current frequency of Holy Communion and Confession, sources of temptation, deficiencies in your habits of prayer, and deficiencies in your faith and your trust in God and your expressions of love for God and neighbor.
- Then, make a list of the ways you could remedy these weaknesses and supply strength in their place

o Fasting, Scripture reading, religious reading, technology fast, Rosary, scheduling Confession, visiting a soup kitchen, etc.

_____
_____
_____
_____
_____
_____
_____
_____
_____
_____
_____
_____

#5. Make an honest assessment of your life at this moment.
- Is there unnecessary discord in your friendships or marriage?
- Are you experiencing odd and recurrent failures of electronics or equipment in your home?
- Does it seem like a "black cloud" follows you around, influencing your life in ways that seem abnormal?
- Do you seem to struggle, without progress, with the same recurrent mortal sins? If so, what steps can you take to resolve any particular issues of the diabolical that may be involved?
- Are you in a state of grace? Is your house blessed? Start there.
- If something still seems to be "off" in your life, move to the binding prayer and consider asking a priest, who is trained in spiritual warfare, for his counsel.[5]

_____

[5] See page 177 for *An Interior Healing Process*

#6. Often, when people are just getting started with spiritual warfare, or are increasing their understanding and attentiveness to the methods of maintaining and increasing spiritual protection, they don't know where to start.
- Go to the *Spiritual Warfare Checklist* on page 169.
- Read through it and be sure you are addressing everything, in order, as mentioned there.
- Use the space below, if helpful, to make any notes or write any insights that come to you in the process.

~ADDITIONAL NOTES FOR THIS SECTION~

Being Strategic in Spiritual Warfare

~PRAYER~

O Beautiful Redeemer,
give me eyes that see Thee,
ears that long for Thy voice,
a mind whose foundation is Thy truths,
and a will that seeks Thee always through holy deeds.
Give me a discerning spirit
that I may always recognize Thy voice
and follow after Thee
shunning the lies and deceit
of the Evil One and his agents.
Inspire me to love goodness, hate evil,
nurture virtue and uproot vice,
to live remembering death so as to die in the embrace of Life,
that the path of my life may not admit
the company of the Deceiver
but may open my soul always to the saving actions of Thy grace.
Amen.

VI: Our Guardian Angels

Patron Saint: St. Frances de Sales

~PRAYER~

O my Jesus,
I give Thee praise for the creation of Thy Holy Angels.
Thy beauty, power, and splendor are magnified by their existence.
Thy love and providence are manifested
through the love and care they give to us.
Our hearts are filled with hope
by knowing of these citizens of Heaven,
whom, by our fidelity to Thy grace,
we will one day see as our brethren.
Let these Holy Angels, assigned to us as guardians,
illuminate our intellects
that we may see if but a glimpse of the glory which they behold
and be ever more zealous in our pursuit of salvation.
Amen.

~INTRODUCTION~

Our Lord's desire to protect us was first revealed in the creation of His holy angels. Among these great creatures, arranged in a hierarchy of nine choirs, were those spirits whom we call Guardian Angels. While they were not the most glorious of the spirits whom God created, they were, nonetheless, exceedingly holy and powerful. Full of grace by their fidelity to God's command, they would be able to assist in the ejection of Satan and the fallen angels from the heavenly realms.

These Guardian Angels, at the moment of their creation, were told that they were to guard and protect a specific individual human person from the moment that person comes into being until they arrive at their eternal reward. These Angels, without hesitation, pledged to fulfill this divine commission fully and faithfully.

From the moment you were brought into being, this individual Angel came to you, fulfilling the mission given to him at his own creation. He loves God perfectly, intensely, and with an undivided will. He will never leave your side but will always protect you and inspire you in the pursuit of goodness to which you are called. The more you call upon his assistance, the more he will be able to give you aid.

Reflections on Sacred Scripture
The following Scripture verses relate to the theme of this section. Read through them slowly, noticing what stands out in each passage. Does a verse convict you of something you are lacking? Does a verse confirm that you are being faithful, thus clearing away doubts? Does a verse strike your heart with a new understanding of God and His holy will?

~~~

~REVELATION 8: 3-4~
Another angel came and stood at the altar with a golden censer; and he was given much incense to mingle with the prayers of all the saints upon the golden altar before the throne; and the smoke of the incense rose with the prayers of the saints from the hand of the angel before God.

~MATTHEW 18:10~
I tell you that in heaven their angels always behold the face of my Father who is in heaven.

~ACTS 8: 26-27~
But an angel of the Lord said to Philip, "Rise and go toward the south to the road that goes down from Jerusalem to Gaza." This is a desert road. And he rose and went.

~ACTS 12: 6-11~
The very night when Herod was about to bring him out, Peter was sleeping between two soldiers, bound with two chains, and sentries before the door were guarding the prison; and behold, an angel of the Lord appeared, and a light shone in the cell; and he struck Peter on the side and woke him, saying, "Get up quickly." And the chains fell off his hands. And the angel said to him, "Dress yourself and put on your sandals." And he did so. And he said to him, "Wrap your mantle around you and follow me." And he went out and followed him; he did not know that what was done by the angel was real, but thought he was seeing a vision. When they had passed the first and the second guard, they came to the iron gate leading into the city. It opened to them of its own accord, and they went out and passed on through one street; and immediately the angel left him. And Peter came to himself, and said, "Now I am sure that the Lord has sent his angel and rescued me from the hand of Herod and from all that the Jewish people were expecting."

~HEBREWS 1:14~
Are they not all ministering spirits sent forth to serve, for the sake of those who are to obtain salvation?

~LUKE 16:22 DR~
And it came to pass, that the beggar died, and was carried by the angels into Abraham's bosom.

~PSALM 33:8 DR~
The angel of the Lord shall encamp round about them that fear him: and shall deliver them.

Our Guardian Angels

~PSALM 91:11~
For he will give his angels charge of you to guard you in all your ways.

~REVELATION 5:11 DR~
And I beheld, and I heard the voice of many angels round about the throne, and the living creatures, and the ancients; and the number of them was thousands of thousands.

~REVELATION 19:10~
Then I fell down at [the angel's] feet to worship him, but he said to me, "You must not do that! I am a fellow servant with you and your brethren who hold the testimony of Jesus. Worship God."

From the Scriptures:
- The holy angels stand in Heaven and on earth constantly interceding for us with God.
- The angels can speak to us, instruct us, liberate us, counsel us, guide us, and encourage us in this life and in our desire to be faithful to Our Lord.
- In life and at death, the angels are there to serve us and to assist us in obtaining salvation.
- Even in dangers, the angels are assigned to us by God to protect us and guard us, we who fear the Lord and walk in His ways.
- The angels are mighty, numerous, and glorious, surrounding and reflecting to us the goodness and glory of God.

As you begin crafting your spiritual warfare Battle Plan, take a moment to process the above verses, and where they may have convicted you regarding your awareness of the assistance of the angels.

1. Do I live with a mind that believes I am accompanied at all times by angels, who, if I call upon them and am faithful to the Lord, are able to protect me and do mighty things in my life?
2. How often do I ponder the beauty, goodness, and power of the holy angels, who will one day be my fellow brethren in Heaven?
3. Do I take time, each day, and throughout my tasks, to call upon my Guardian Angel, and to thank him for the great and small things I have noticed him do to aid me?

_____

_____

_____

_____

_____

_____

Slaying Dragons – Prepare for Battle

Our Guardian Angels

~PONDERANCE~

In our families and in our friendships, we look to each other for support and encouragement. We are comforted by the voices we hear and the smiles we can see. We are aided by the strength and protection which these friends can supply. All of this takes place in the visible world which Our Lord created.

As men of faith, we also know and believe that there is an invisible world which Our Lord also created. We profess it at least weekly in the Creed, we acknowledge it at Holy Mass and in our devotions, and we hear it proclaimed by the priest in nearly every rite of blessing or Sacrament given to us by the Church.

Yet, for so many, that invisible world is lost to us, locked away behind the veil which separates us from God, only to be torn away at death. This, though, does not change the reality – the invisible world is still there, and the powers of God and His goodness are there, waiting for us to call upon them.

Our Guardian Angels are part of this invisible world, which we too often lose sight of. If we live as if the invisible world does not exist, we will be living within a great ignorance! St. Alphonsus, in describing a man's final Judgment, mentions that, after Satan comes forward to accuse him, his Guardian Angel will present evidence of how he labored for the man's salvation, and how his warnings were ignored.

A practical denial of the invisible world, whereby we profess it to exist but we ignore all that it contains, risks turning our faith in God into a superstition, leaving us vulnerable to the diabolical which will take advantage of this blindness, and placing us on the battlefield of life without the powerful protection God intended for us to have – our Guardian Angels.

It is not of God to choose to restrict our vision of life to that which is accessible to the senses alone. We must challenge this aspect of the modern world which daily attempts to creep into our minds and hearts. By embracing this skewed perspective, we cut ourselves off from powerful friends and holy allies!

Imagine the indescribable and immense hierarchy of angels, like the highest mountain, through which the glory of God permeates and descends, like the falls of the greatest river, intending to reach us with the sound of a myriad of angelic voices calling out the praises of the Lord. These voices desire to touch our souls and invigorate us with the truth of our divine vocation – that we are all called to be, through Baptism, truly the sons and daughters of God!

The angels long to look upon us by their side in eternal splendor, and work tirelessly to bring us there, offering us a thousand graces and aids to do so. We must allow them to supply for our needs on earth, as the Lord has willed, and as has been revealed time and time again in the pages of Sacred Scripture. Take the hand of your Guardian Angel and let him lead you along the way.

Slaying Dragons – Prepare for Battle

A reminder of some essential points, from *Slaying Dragons*...

+ The first thought of our Guardian Angels was that they wanted to serve God by protecting us.
+ Our Guardian Angels said "yes," without hesitation, to God's call to them to protect us in this life, and they continue to do so.
+ In addition to Our Lady and the saints, Catholics should nurture a devotion to and a friendship with their Guardian Angels, who are much more powerful than most people realize.
+ According to St. Thomas Aquinas, a man's guardian angel is more powerful than even the Devil himself.
+ After their "yes," the angels were sealed in sanctifying grace and granted entrance into the Beatific Vision, where they behold God constantly, face to face.
+ The demons are not in possession of the kind and amount and depth of knowledge as are the angels who are faithful to the Lord.
+ Our Guardian Angels, from the lowest choir in the angelic hierarchy, are more powerful than Satan, which must force us to reflect on the power and holiness of those in the higher choirs.
+ Those who have entered into a vocation (religious life, priesthood, married life) have been given an additional angel to protect that vocation.
+ Our Guardian Angels are assigned to us by divine decree; they neither can nor will ever leave us in this life.
+ Angels are capable of influencing our souls and our bodies in a variety of ways, which include not only holy inspirations but also the calming of our passions and the healing of our bodies.
+ Angels enjoy the possession of divinely infused knowledge, and are incomparably more intelligent than men, possessing an intellectual clarity and a capacity to know more than we do.
+ Angels have the ability to block and to undo all the work of the demons.

Questions to consider:
- Would you say that you have a relationship and a friendship with your Guardian Angel?
- When you call upon your Guardian Angel for assistance, do you see him as he truly is, a mighty and holy being who has dedicated himself, without flaw, to serving you?
- In times when you are afraid, or worried, or in a fearful situation, do you believe that your Guardian Angel will protect you, or does he not come to mind at all?

_____

_____

_____

_____

_____

Our Guardian Angels

~CONSIDERATIONS~

#1. The knowledge in the intellect of a demon is tremendous, but knowledge is not more powerful than grace. While Satan is higher by nature, our Guardian Angels are stronger through grace. Consider:
- What could your Guardian Angel do for you when your mind is being turned toward sin by the strong pressure of a diabolical temptation?
- What would you <u>like</u> for your Guardian Angel to do for you in your daily routine, according to what he is capable of doing?
- Are there certain kinds of assistance you need or could use that your Guardian Angel can do and which you can begin to ask him about?

Make a list of the ways in which you would like your Guardian Angel to help you. Then, take some time to speak to him about this.

_____
_____
_____
_____
_____
_____
_____
_____
_____
_____
_____
_____
_____
_____
_____
_____
_____

Our Guardian Angels

#2. Take comfort in the fact that, while we struggle to discern God's will, in our vocation and in our day-to-day living, the Holy Angels do not. They directly perceive God's will and understand it completely. They then consent to it fully.
- Ask your Guardian Angel to help you understand, and consent to, God's will in a similar manner. The Angels can obtain "light" for your intellect, as the famous prayer to them states.[1]
- What are the concrete things about God's will that you desire to understand better?

_____
_____
_____
_____
_____
_____
_____
_____
_____
_____
_____
_____

#3. Knowing the power of the angelic nature to influence us, re-dedicate yourself to your Guardian Angel, and give him permission to act in your life. You can even ask him to heal you and strengthen you in ways that you are in need.
- Take some time to craft your own prayer to your Guardian Angel, telling him exactly what you specifically need his help with.
- Add the things you listed in the above Consideration.

_____
_____
_____

---

[1] See page 223 for the *Prayer to Guardian Angel*

#4. The power and perfection of the angelic intellect is something that our Guardian Angels possess as well. If you do not already do so, start nurturing the habit of praying to your Guardian Angel all throughout your days. He loves you and desires to do so much in your life, if you let him. God acts in the same way.
- Note the times in the day when it would be good and easy for you to remember the presence of your Guardian Angel.
- When you pray to your Guardian Angel, do you speak to him with a confidence that demonstrates you understand his power, perfection, and beauty?
- Remember to honor and celebrate your Guardian Angel on his feast day, October 2nd.

Our Guardian Angels

#5. Entrust yourself completely to your Guardian Angel. Pray the traditional "Angel of God" prayer devoutly, slowly, intentionally, and sincerely. Do so knowing that you are speaking to an angelic person, who is listening, loving, very powerful, and dedicated to serving you and getting you to Heaven.

#6. While Angels cannot see the future, their knowledge of all that is happening everywhere is immense. Keep this in mind when speaking with your Guardian Angel. The Holy Angels can communicate with each other easily, and Guardian Angels can speak to other Guardian Angels.
- Did you know you can send him on "missions" and ask him to help you with things that concern your day-to-day life, such as meetings with people?
- What tasks could you ask your Guardian Angel to do that would bring real relief to your life? Think about that, do it with faith, and then see what happens.[2]

---

[2] These conversations with our Guardian Angel are always with humility, not seeking power or secret knowledge, but simply aid and understanding, which can involve helping you know certain things about the world, but always within God's laws.

Slaying Dragons – Prepare for Battle

~ADDITIONAL NOTES FOR THIS SECTION~

Our Guardian Angels

~Prayer~

O Holy Angel of God,
my friend, my guardian, my companion,
you are a sure sign of God's love
and His desire that I walk this pilgrimage safely
and come to my promised reward in Heaven.
As you once accepted me as God's assigned task for you,
so now I restate that I accept you as God's assigned protector for me.
Stay with me all the day through.
Never leave my side.
Whisper reminders of your presence often.
Teach me the ways in which you can help.
Shield me from the assaults of the Enemy,
and help me to overcome myself,
that I may one day give you the thanks that you deserve
when I see you face to face in the glory of Heaven.
Amen.

VII: Gratitude for God's Protection

Patron Saint: St. Rita of Cascia

~PRAYER~

I give Thee thanks, Almighty Father,
for the infinite power and love which you turn toward us
that we might be saved.
There is nothing in this universe
which can prevent us from obtaining Thy goodness and love,
nothing save ourselves.
Let me see, O Sovereign Lord,
the presence of Thy gentle hand in my life,
the pierced hand of my Redeemer,
whose victory has astonished the powers of darkness
and set free the captives it had held bound.
I give Thee thanks, Lord of Heaven and earth,
that nothing in the heavens nor on the earth can take me away from Thee.
I surrender all my fears to Thee, that Thou wilt replace them with Thy promises.
I long to hear the Angels sing of the victory of the Lamb,
and of all who have washed their robes in His Sacred Blood.
Cover me, Lord, with Thy Precious Blood, and I will be free.
Amen.

~INTRODUCTION~

When we are Baptized and brought into the Eternal Covenant, we are granted many promises from Our Lord. All of these can be summed up in Our Lord's statement: "Take My yoke upon you and learn from Me; for I am gentle and lowly in heart, and you will find rest for your souls. For my yoke is easy, and my burden is light."[1]

This promise of rest comes immediately after His explanation that the Father reveals His truths to the little ones who are humble, not the wise and the learned. It is to those who trust Him, and rely on Him, and surrender to Him, that experience His protection, His blessing, and His peace.

---

[1] Matthew 11:29-30

Slaying Dragons – Prepare for Battle

Reflections on Sacred Scripture

The following Scripture verses relate to the theme of this section. Read through them slowly, noticing what stands out in each passage. Does a verse convict you of something you are lacking? Does a verse confirm that you are being faithful, thus clearing away doubts? Does a verse strike your heart with a new understanding of God and His holy will?

~~~

~ISAIAH 41: 10-13~
Fear not, for I am with you, be not dismayed, for I am your God; I will strengthen you, I will help you, I will uphold you with my victorious right hand. Behold, all who are incensed against you shall be put to shame and confounded; those who strive against you shall be as nothing and shall perish. You shall seek those who contend with you, but you shall not find them; those who war against you shall be as nothing at all. For I, the LORD your God, hold your right hand; it is I who say to you, "Fear not, I will help you."

~PROVERBS 18:10~
The name of the LORD is a strong tower; the righteous man runs into it and is safe.

~1 CORINTHIANS 1:4~
I give thanks to God always for you because of the grace of God which was given you in Christ Jesus.

~2 KINGS 6:16~
The servant of Eliseus was struck with terror when he saw the city encompassed with enemies; but the saint inspired him with courage, saying, 'Fear not; for there are more with us than with them.' He then showed him an army of angels sent by God to defend the city.[2]

~ROMANS 8:31~
What then shall we say to this? If God is for us, who is against us?

~2 THESSALONIANS 3:3-4~
The Lord is faithful; he will strengthen you and guard you from evil. And we have confidence in the Lord about you, that you are doing and will do the things which we command.

~2 TIMOTHY 4:18 DR~
The Lord hath delivered me from every evil work: and will preserve me unto his heavenly kingdom, to whom be glory for ever and ever. Amen.

~PSALM 121:7-8~
The LORD will keep you from all evil; he will keep your life. The LORD will keep your going out and your coming in from this time forth and for evermore.

---

[2] Quote here from St. Alphonsus Liguori, *Preparation for Death*, p98; as in *Slaying Dragons*, p151, ref. the verse cited.

Gratitude for God's Protection

~PSALM 91:1-2~
He who dwells in the shelter of the Most High, who abides in the shadow of the Almighty, will say to the LORD, "My refuge and my fortress; my God, in whom I trust."

~2 SAMUEL 22:3-4~
My God, my rock, in whom I take refuge, my shield and the horn of my salvation, my stronghold and my refuge, my savior; thou savest me from violence. I call upon the LORD, who is worthy to be praised, and I am saved from my enemies.

~PSALM 5:11~
Let all who take refuge in thee rejoice, let them ever sing for joy; and do thou defend them, that those who love thy name may exult in thee.

~PSALM 46:1~
God is our refuge and strength, a very present help in trouble.

~NAHUM 1:7~
The LORD is good, a stronghold in the day of trouble; he knows those who take refuge in him.

~PROVERBS 30:5~
Every word of God proves true; he is a shield to those who take refuge in him.

~PSALM 3:3~
Thou, O LORD, art a shield about me, my glory, and the lifter of my head.

From the Scriptures:
- Our Lord repeats and reassures us that He is always present to help us, and to strengthen us, and to scatter our enemies.
- When we seek righteousness and abide in His grace, we will receive the supernatural helps and protections we long for and are promised.
- Having delivered us from evil, the Lord will preserve us in His grace and guide us into His heavenly kingdom.
- If we take refuge in God, we find in Him a strong fortress and foundation, a place of peace and security, a place of protection and life.
- The Lord knows those who take refuge in Him and lifts up their heads with a supply of hope and courage.

As you begin crafting your spiritual warfare Battle Plan, take a moment to process the above verses, and where they may have convicted you regarding the confidence you place in Our Lord's love.
1. When I pray, do I look to the Lord as a source of strength, love, and comfort?
2. When my prayers include petitions for help in the midst of fear and trial, do I look to God as a reliable and powerful refuge in which I may truly take my rest despite my troubles?
3. Would others regard me as one who rides the storms of life in a manner that reveals a deep and abiding trust in Our Lord's protection?

Slaying Dragons – Prepare for Battle

Gratitude for God's Protection

~PONDERANCE~

Often, when we are distracted by our worldly cares and filled with anxieties unrelated to our salvation, we forget that this world is a battlefield where that same salvation is the treasure over which dueling armies fight. As a result, we become forgetful about the extent to which Our Lord has gone, and goes every day, to ensure and protect that salvation. This forgetfulness will lead to greater and abiding anxiety if we do not seek to remedy it by assiduous prayer and spiritual vigilance.

The Church teaches us firmly that the demons are not capable, on their own, of stealing us away from God. While instilling fear in us is one of the goals of the diabolic, this fear is easily countered by a reliance on Christ's grace. Grace and humility, trust and faith, will bind us to God in such a way that the demons will then appear as pathetic little barking dogs, incapable of harming us. Recall the power of Our Lady and the Saints: those who are bound to Christ are instruments of victory over Satan.

Remember the verse above, from 2 Kings 6:16. Here, the King of Syria comes out against Elisha since Elisha had been thwarting the plans of the King of Syria against Israel. When the army of Syria arrived and surrounded the city where they dwelt, the servant of Elisha was filled with fear. Elisha calmed him with a statement of wisdom: "Fear not, for those who are with us are more than those who are with them."

The prophet of the Lord then prayed, asking God to open the eyes of the servant, that he might see and understand what the prophet knew as a result of his holiness and union with God – that the mountain where they stood was filled with horses and chariots of fire – angels. These angels then struck the entire army blind at the request of Elisha, who then led them off to the King of Israel as captives.

When we are faithful to the Lord, He will fight for us and will win mighty victories in our lives. When we struggle, we must call upon the assistance of the Communion of Saints, those holy men and women who, like Elisha, can help us understand and who can obtain for us God's graces.

We must be grateful, then, always, for the fact that Our Lord has created a world where all is positioned in our favor. There are more angels than demons. Christ has already conquered Satan, sin, and death. If we hold fast to the love and mercy of Christ, we will be saved. Fear not. Love God and live well. Become holy and the demons will tuck their tails and flee in the opposite direction.

A reminder of some essential points, from *Slaying Dragons*...

+ Our Lord has complete control over the demons. They are only allowed to do what He permits them to do.
+ The Church possesses both power and authority over the diabolical. This power over demons can increase based on the holiness of the individual priest.
+ In almost all cases of mortal sin, God blocks the demons from proceeding with possession, as He does with most cases of general diabolical activity, blocking the demons from doing what they would prefer to do to us.
+ Demons do whatever God will allow them to do. God does allow them to act, though within the limits that He sets.
+ The power of the demons is limited in part due to the absence of sanctifying grace, which also limits their understanding of God's plan and leads them to make mistakes.
+ Sacred Scripture, the lives of the saints, and the work of exorcists demonstrate the reality of this limitation on diabolical activity.
+ The demons fear everything that points to God or has been sanctified by its union with Him, especially the Holy Name of Jesus and the invocation of the Most Precious Blood of Jesus.
+ The sacramentals, such as holy water, blessed candles, or a blessed crucifix, will frustrate and block the work of demons.
+ Our Lady, infused with sanctifying grace from the moment of her conception, is a remarkably powerful force against the demonic.

Questions to consider:
- Do you take for granted the protection God is constantly supplying for you, particularly the times in which you have gone astray and placed yourself in danger of the Enemy's attacks?
- When you are discouraged or are tempted to stop praying or trusting God's goodness, do you call to mind the evidence of His love and protection that He has provided, such as the numerous Sacraments, sacramentals, blessings, prayers, and sources and stories of healing and strength and miracles?
- Have you constructed a routine to remind you to daily call upon Our Lord and the Communion of Saints in the many ways the Church has suggested, so that you may abide securely, each day, in the mighty fortress of His peace?
    o Perhaps you could link a certain prayer to your morning cup of coffee, before a nap, during your lunch, etc.

Gratitude for God's Protection

Slaying Dragons – Prepare for Battle

~CONSIDERATIONS~

#1. We all experience some amount of fear throughout our lives. Think about the amount of fear you experience in your daily life and the way it speaks to you and controls your behavior.
- How much fear do you experience in your day-to-day living?
- Does it feel like the fear has a life of its own and you cannot "turn it off"?

Analyze this carefully. Write down your fears and then look at them again.
- Are some of them easy to remedy or eliminate?

_____
_____
_____
_____
_____
_____
_____
_____
_____
_____
_____
_____
_____
_____
_____
_____
_____
_____
_____

Gratitude for God's Protection

#2. Fear originates from a source. These sources are detectable upon reflection. Our Lord repeatedly states, "Fear not," so we must seek to surrender all fears to Him and be at peace.
- Where is it coming from?
- Are there sources of this fear that you have control over?
- Do some of them feel beyond your control?

Analyze all of your fears and make a plan to eliminate those sources of fear over which you have control, like music or videos or shows that you view regularly, too little exercise or fresh air, or too much sugar or caffeine or tobacco which keeps you edgy and anxious. Then, see what remains and determine what you need in order to calm those further fears.
- Do you need to go to Confession, Mass, prayer, on a retreat, or get spiritual advice from a good priest related to these fears and any connected sins or vices?
- Would seeking a Catholic psychologist or a doctor also be helpful?

#3. Consider the times when you have been depressed or anxious or suffered from some sort of illness.
- What impact did this have on your faith and life of prayer?
- Did it push you away from God, prayer, a Sacramental life, or a life of grace?
- Did it cause you to forget God's blessings or even distrust His desire to save you?
- Or did it cause you to draw closer to Our Lord, growing in confidence in His Love?

If it has had a negative impact, those moments made you more vulnerable to sin, doubt, and diabolical influence. Consider whether there is more spiritual work that you need to do to fully heal and strengthen your soul from the battle it has been through.
- Do you have lingering doubts about God's goodness?
- Do you hold back on going to Confession out of shame of some past sin?
- Are you angry at the course your life has taken, or took at some point, which interferes with your ability to pray well?

Take some time to sit in God's presence and ask Him to protect you and liberate you from your fears. Use a moment that captivates your attention: a sunset, a walk, time in Adoration, the beach or mountains. Consider having a meal with friends to share stories of God's protection.

Gratitude for God's Protection

~ADDITIONAL NOTES FOR THIS SECTION~

Slaying Dragons – Prepare for Battle

~PRAYER~

Humbly I beseech Thee, my God,
to pardon the many times
when I have doubted Thy goodness,
held bitterness in my heart
or anger against Thee.
For, in the mystery of Thy ways,
I often did not see, nor understand,
the mighty works Thy Providence performs,
daily tending and daily defending
Thy wayward sheep.
Take me up, O Gentle Shepherd,
let me rest upon Thy strength.
In my surrender, I trust,
Thou wilt give me blessed peace and happiness.
Amen.

VIII: Our Thoughts

Patron Saint: St. Pio of Pietrelcina

~PRAYER~

Deliver me, O Lord,
from every thought of doubt and despair,
of envy and dissatisfaction,
of worry and distrust in Thy Providence,
and those thoughts which constantly recall
the sins of my wayward days.
Instill in my mind,
by the fire of Thy Holy Spirit,
the vivifying Truth of Thy Love and Goodness,
the beauty of Thy Saints and the Halls of Heaven,
the salvific power of suffering and Thy Holy Cross,
and the wonder and majesty of all Thy ways and works.
Capture and captivate my mind, O Lord,
that I may seek and desire all Truth and wisdom that comes from Thee.
Amen.

~INTRODUCTION~

Our mind is a most precious aspect of our being. It is the seat of rationality, the core of our dignity as persons, the location in which we encounter God and His sacred Truths. It is here that we become formed into the person we will be for all eternity, for it is here that we store up the knowledge from which we then elect to act. Faith is the supernatural assent of the intellect to all the Truths revealed by God through His Church. In our intellect, we ponder the sacred mysteries and, by faith, give our assent and believe them to be true.

In the writings of Pope St. Gregory the Great on the life of St. Benedict, we are reminded that grace infused into the soul is destined to unite our thoughts with Our Lord's. For, as St. Gregory says, "Holy men do know the Lord's thoughts, in so far as they are one with Him."[1] St. Paul adds, "Now we have received not the spirit of this world, but the Spirit that is of God; that we may know the things that are given us from God."[2] Let the Holy Spirit fill and purify our thoughts, that we may know and be pleasing to Him.

---

[1] *Life and Miracles of St. Benedict* Liturgical Press, 1949, p 40
[2] 1 Corinthians 2:12

Reflections on Sacred Scripture
The following Scripture verses relate to the theme of this section. Read through them slowly, noticing what stands out in each passage. Does a verse convict you of something you are lacking? Does a verse confirm that you are being faithful, thus clearing away doubts? Does a verse strike your heart with a new understanding of God and His holy will?

~~~

~ROMANS 12:2~
Do not be conformed to this world but be transformed by the renewal of your mind, that you may prove what is the will of God, what is good and acceptable and perfect.

~1 CORINTHIANS 3:18-20~
Let no one deceive himself. If any one among you thinks that he is wise in this age, let him become a fool that he may become wise. For the wisdom of this world is folly with God. For it is written, "He catches the wise in their craftiness," and again, "The Lord knows that the thoughts of the wise are futile."

~PROVERBS 4:20-23~
My son, be attentive to my words; incline your ear to my sayings. Let them not escape from your sight; keep them within your heart. For they are life to him who finds them, and healing to all his flesh. Keep your heart with all vigilance; for from it flow the springs of life.

~COLOSSIANS 3:2,5~
Set your minds on things that are above, not on things that are on earth. Put to death therefore what is earthly in you: immorality, impurity, passion, evil desire, and covetousness, which is idolatry.

~MATTHEW 15:18-19~
But what comes out of the mouth proceeds from the heart, and this defiles a man. For out of the heart come evil thoughts, murder, adultery, fornication, theft, false witness, slander.

~PHILIPPIANS 4:8-9~
Finally, brethren, whatever is true, whatever is honorable, whatever is just, whatever is pure, whatever is lovely, whatever is gracious, if there is any excellence, if there is anything worthy of praise, think about these things. What you have learned and received and heard and seen in me, do; and the God of peace will be with you.

~PROVERBS 3:5~
Trust in the LORD with all your heart, and do not rely on your own insight.

~MATTHEW 21:22~
Whatever you ask in prayer, you will receive, if you have faith.

Our Thoughts

~PSALM 139:1-2~
O LORD, thou hast searched me and known me! Thou knowest when I sit down and when I rise up; thou discernest my thoughts from afar.

~ISAIAH 55:8~
For my thoughts are not your thoughts, neither are your ways my ways, says the LORD.

~ISAIAH 11:3-4~
He shall not judge by what his eyes see, or decide by what his ears hear; but with righteousness he shall judge the poor, and decide with equity for the meek of the earth

From the Scriptures:
- Our thoughts must be configured to the mind of Christ and the laws of God, to the revelation of Truth that has come from the Almighty.
- Our minds must be consumed with the thoughts of what is above, for what is on earth is deadly and what is above gives life.
- It is from man's core, his heart, that all decisions are made; he must, therefore, set his heart on all that is good and holy, that his actions may proceed from this.
- The Lord reads the heart, and knows all our longings, and answers us when we call upon Him with faith.
- We must take for ourselves the mind of Christ, that we may see as God sees, and think as God thinks, that we may love as He loves, and live where He lives.

As you begin crafting your spiritual warfare Battle Plan, take a moment to process the above verses, and where they may have convicted you regarding the importance of the pattern of our thoughts.
1. In what ways do you configure your mind to the mind and will of God?
2. Do you monitor your internal and secret thoughts, sifting through them constantly, and separating and condemning what is not of God?
3. Is your heart set on God, seeking to be pleasing to Him in all things, and to seek and dedicate yourself only to those things which point to, or flow from, Him?

_____

_____

_____

_____

_____

_____

Slaying Dragons – Prepare for Battle

Our Thoughts

~PONDERANCE~

The three primary influences of evil are the world, the flesh, and the devil. To these three influences we are subject our entire lives. Each of these exerts a pull on our minds and on our wills. The world champions, and makes easy and rewarding, the life of sin and selfishness and pride. The flesh champions, and makes easy and pleasurable, the life of greed and desire and curiosity for evil. The devil champions and encourages, the life of indulgence and self-worship and forgetfulness of God.

This bombardment of influence impacts every one of us, even those destined, like St. Therese, toward quick and intense holiness. There is no place to hide from the influence – the call, instead, is to fortify ourselves internally that we may endure the assaults without being convinced to compromise on our fidelity to the Lord.

St. Ignatius of Loyola, renowned for his articulation of the discernment of spirits, experienced the power of grace and power of the fallen flesh to influence his mind and heart in different ways. Restricted to his bed as he recovered from an injury, he read over both the novels of the day, which he had long enjoyed, as well as Sacred Scripture and the lives of the Saints. As he moved from one text to the other, he became very much aware of a drastically different impact which these concepts, as presented by the books, these stories of valor or vainglory, had on his soul.

The desires of his heart were moved in one manner toward the things of the earth, and by another toward the things of Heaven. Quickly, he laid aside the selfish pursuits of the old man, which left him empty and inclined toward worldliness, and took up his cross, inclining himself toward the way of Christ, in which he found life and freedom and holiness.

Our thoughts lead us in a direction, and down a path to an end. There is no thought which can be regarded as morally neutral, for all are pointing us toward truth or falsehood, selflessness or selfishness, virtue or vice.

Our call, as Christians, is, as St. Paul states, to "be transformed by the renewal of your mind,"[3] turning aside from what is base and temporal and embracing with the entire spirit the revelation of the glory of God and the path to salvation. This, as should be expected for those who are "born for combat,"[4] is the work of a hero, of a lover of God, of a man who has died with Christ and no longer lives his earthly life but who can say, with St. Paul, "I have been crucified with Christ; it is no longer I who live, but Christ who lives in me; and the life I now live in the flesh I live by faith in the Son of God, who loved me and gave himself for me."[5]

---

[3] Romans 12:2
[4] Pope Leo XIII, *Sapientiae Christianae*, 14
[5] Galatians 2:20

A reminder of some essential points, from *Slaying Dragons*...

+ The first place of temptation is the intellect, which makes mental prayer and meditation, which fill the mind with sacred images and ideas, and block the work of demons, to be of extreme value.
+ Demons cleverly impart thoughts into our minds in ways that are nearly impossible to detect.
+ Sometimes the demons will attack the mind, overwhelming it with ideas and images, in order to break the will and move the person to sin.
+ When our minds and thoughts are ordered toward God, demons will be less inclined to tempt us.
+ When demons do tempt one who prays often, that person is more equipped to detect the presence of the temptation and dismiss it as such.
+ Angels communicate with one another by acting on the intellect of another angel. They, and the demons, can act on our intellects in the same way.

Thoughts to consider:
- The renewal of the mind which St. Paul calls us to seek is attainable by another command: "pray without ceasing."
- Custody of the mind is vital in protecting our entire being, for all evil enters here and then seeks to disorder the rest of our nature.
- When the mind is focused on God, constantly recalling His law and love, the demons are unable to effectively influence us and their temptations come to little or nothing.

Our Thoughts

~CONSIDERATIONS~

#1. Do I ever find myself attached to sinful desires such as pride, revenge, and a rejection of being merciful toward others? If so, reflect upon the fact that, in these sins, your desires are beginning to resemble those of the demons, who are principally animated by pride. If you are inclined to think that this is not true, merely because you never notice any activity of the diabolical in your life, remember that, if you are already thinking and acting like them, they may be leaving you alone for a reason.

___

#2. Most people in the world, including people within the Church, do not have a proper belief regarding the reality of the devil. Some reject the teaching completely while others are afraid of the devil. Analyze your own thinking in this regard.
- Do I think it is silly to be concerned about temptation, or the activity of the devil, or the ability of the devil to influence the wider world?
- Do you fear talking about or speaking about anything having to do with the devil, from a desire to avoid being on his "radar" or drawing an attack from him?

Slaying Dragons – Prepare for Battle

#3. Does the fact that demons can have access to all of your memories, and can summon them to your mind whenever they want, cause you alarm? It should at least cause you to stop and think. This is another reason to avoid looking at immoral and violent images, far too accessible today. These images are traumatic to the conscience. Placing them into our memories is doing the demons a favor.

- Which areas in your life, such as rooms, cars, and computers, can you place sacred images, which, by their constant presence, will become embedded in your memory and imagination?

_____

_____

_____

_____

_____

_____

_____

#4. One recommended practice is to ask God to help you forget the evils that you have experienced and which are tied to particular wounds you carry. This forgetfulness will disarm the diabolical and limit the arsenal they have at their disposal, as they will not be able to dredge up things from your past. Make a list of the evils that you have seen, heard, or experienced and which continue to appear in your life from time to time. Surrender these to Our Lord and ask Him to help you forget them completely.[6]

- There are some good prayers for healing of wounds and memory in *Deliverance Prayers for Use by the Laity*, by Fr. Ripperger

_____

_____

_____

_____

_____

[6] Consider using this list as part of the *Interior Healing Process* on page 177, for which you would write these on a separate sheet of paper to be burned.

Our Thoughts

#5. Christians are called to think the best of others and presume they have good intentions until it is proven otherwise. This eliminates proud thinking on our part, which would condemn people we do not understand or would incline us to feel offended at what may have been simply a poor, or emotion-driven, choice of words. "Bless those who curse you," as Our Lord commands.
- Consider your typical daily and weekly activities and the times you are often tempted to hastily condemn someone and their motives.
- Do these thoughts proceed from reason and charity or from pride and anger?
- Are there other factors which have caused you to be unsettled and, thus, inclined to rash judgment?
- When a person offends you, what thought manifests in your mind? Is it of judgment and anger, a rush to judgment or pausing to assume the person truly has a good intention?
- Try to resist reacting strongly or quickly when offended or opposed or insulted. Instead, process it internally in the form of a prayer, a conversation with Our Lord.
    - o Does this bring a more general decrease in anxiety or opposition against others, and make it easier to interact pleasantly with others?
- See the *Litany of Humility* on page 231, which would be helpful here.

#6. Our reason, memory, and imagination are targets of the demons in order to influence us and tempt us toward evil. What are some ways in which you could work to further block their ability to use these three avenues against you?
- Do you study the Faith sufficiently to eradicate doubt?
- Have you uprooted enduring vices which are tied to sins from your past?
- Have you ended your use of immoral or violent images and filled your day with sacred images, either from holy cards and icons or daily meditation on the life of Christ?

Our Thoughts

_____

#7. Consider the clarity with which your mind operates.
- Are you easily swayed to think about certain things which are sinful, such as lust, revenge, anger, or indulgence?
- Do you feel inclined toward thoughts of despair, depression, fear, anxiety, mistrust, death, or a desire to escape from your life?
- Do these thoughts appear in a pattern, or predictably, and burden you in such a way that you find yourself taking the same sins to Confession over and over again without making progress in the virtues that oppose those sins?
    o If so, there may be a spiritual issue to resolve.

First, consider whether depression or another mental burden is the natural explanation. Then, consider further whether it could be a mild, or strong, case of diabolical obsession. The Sacraments, sacramentals, binding prayers, mental prayer and meditation (the Rosary), and, if necessary, the prayers of a priest will help break the diabolical obsession if it is present. The increased spiritual work will thwart the devil's attacks even if the problem is simply the cross of ordinary temptation.

_____

#8. Consider beginning your evening, as the day slows and points to its end, with the *Suscipe* prayer of St. Ignatius, at the end of this section.

Slaying Dragons – Prepare for Battle

~ADDITIONAL NOTES FOR THIS SECTION~

Our Thoughts

~PRAYER~

Take, Lord, and receive
all my liberty,
my memory, my understanding,
and my entire will,
All I have and call my own.
You have given all to me.
To You, Lord, I return it.
Everything is Yours; do with it what You will.
Give me only Your love and Your grace,
that is enough for me.
-
Suscipe, by St. Ignatius of Loyola

IX: Temptation

Patron Saint: St. Thomas Aquinas

~PRAYER~

Lead me, O Lord,
and teach me Thy Word,
that I may recognize Thy Voice,
and follow after Thee.
Grant me the gift to discern my thoughts,
separating those that are evil
from those that lead to Thee.
Unmask the attempts of the Enemy to seduce me, lead me astray,
and manipulate my understanding.
Heal my wounds and clear my memories of evil and sadness.
Grant me a renewed vision of the gift of life Thou hast given to me,
that my heart will always long to see this life fulfilled
in fidelity and obedience to Thee.
Amen.

~INTRODUCTION~

The trial of temptation is the chief cross that all men must carry. The lives of the great Saints make it clear that resisting temptation, more than martyrdom, more than being an illuminated author, more than making thousands of converts, is the path to salvation.

When St. Ignatius saw the emptiness of a life of sin and vanity, he embraced a period of intense penance to purify his soul. St. Francis, likewise, when setting off into the Lord's service, was quick to punish his wayward flesh to cure it of its evil passions. St. Thomas Aquinas promptly dismissed the harlot sent to lure him to sin and to abandon his calling, thus acquiring the gift of perfect chastity as a reward.

We must look to the Saints for inspiration, for their stories tell of the heroic nature of daily Christian living. When a Christian puts God first, his life will not become easy, but his faith will endure in times of trial, and shine in the heat of battle. Like the Saints, we must be willing to remove, even with great penance, our evil inclinations. They prove that, with God, this effort will produce the holy fruit we desire. Too often, the devil tempts us to think that our efforts of prayer and penance, while pleasing to the Lord, will never produce real strength. The Saints prove this to be a lie.

Reflections on Sacred Scripture

The following Scripture verses relate to the theme of this section. Read through them slowly, noticing what stands out in each passage. Does a verse convict you of something you are lacking? Does a verse confirm that you are being faithful, thus clearing away doubts? Does a verse strike your heart with a new understanding of God and His holy will?

~~~

~1 CORINTHIANS 10:13~
No temptation has overtaken you that is not common to man. God is faithful, and he will not let you be tempted beyond your strength, but with the temptation will also provide the way of escape, that you may be able to endure it.

~DEUTERONOMY 8:1-3~
And you shall remember all the way which the LORD your God has led you these forty years in the wilderness, that he might humble you, testing you to know what was in your heart, whether you would keep his commandments, or not.

~MATTHEW 26:41~
Watch [*keep awake*] and pray that you may not enter into temptation; the spirit indeed is willing, but the flesh is weak.

~2 CORINTHIANS 11:3~
But I am afraid that as the serpent deceived Eve by his cunning, your thoughts will be led astray from a sincere and pure devotion to Christ.

~MARK 7:20-23~
What comes out of a man is what defiles a man. For from within, out of the heart of man, come evil thoughts… All these evil things come from within, and they defile a man.

~JAMES 1:13-15~
Let no one say when he is tempted, "I am tempted by God"; for God cannot be tempted with evil and he himself tempts no one; but each person is tempted when he is lured and enticed by his own desire. Then desire when it has conceived gives birth to sin; and sin when it is full-grown brings forth death.

~PROVERBS 7:25-27~
Let not your heart turn aside to her ways, do not stray into her paths; for many a victim has she laid low; yea, all her slain are a mighty host. Her house is the way to Sheol, going down to the chambers of death.

~1 TIMOTHY 6:9~
But those who desire to be rich fall into temptation, into a snare, into many senseless and hurtful desires that plunge men into ruin and destruction.

Temptation

~1 PETER 4:12~
Beloved, do not be surprised at the fiery ordeal which comes upon you to prove you, as though something strange were happening to you.

~JAMES 1:12~
Blessed is the man who endures trial, for when he has stood the test he will receive the crown of life which God has promised to those who love him.

From the Scriptures:
- God permits the temptations that come to us, but none are outside of what all men endure, nor too strong to resist.
- If we trust in God, the devil's temptations will appear as they truly are, and we will have the wit to refuse to enter them; but the Enemy is crafty, so we must not let our thoughts go astray.
- Our evil desires are what defile us, when we by our evil choosing, seek after sin, taking the way by which many fall: the path that leads to death.
- We will all pass through the trials of temptation, but those who love God, and who persevere through them, will merit the reward of eternal life.

As you begin crafting your spiritual warfare Battle Plan, take a moment to process the above verses, and where they may have convicted you regarding how careful you are with temptation.
1. Do you complain to the Lord that the temptations you endure are unfair and too strong for you?
2. Are you doing enough to stabilize your soul so, when the temptations come, you are prepared to endure them effectively?
3. Do you have a heart that is willing to suffer all the trials that this life brings, knowing that it will bring you into a deeper union with Our Lord in this life, and greater glory in the life to come?

_____

_____

_____

_____

_____

_____

_____

Slaying Dragons – Prepare for Battle

Temptation

~PONDERANCE~

St. Jean Vianney counsels us, "We are all inclined to sin, my children; we are idle, greedy, sensual, given to the pleasures of the flesh. We want to know everything, to learn everything, to see everything; we must watch over our mind, over our heart, over our senses, for these are the gates by which the devil penetrates. See, he prowls round us incessantly; his only occupation in this world is to seek companions for himself."[1]

The life of the soul, when weakness is allowed to remain and the heroic penances of the Saints are not embraced, is like a tempest; the winds rarely cease, the waves continue to crash, and the debris is scattered throughout, including the seeds of evil desire placed by the Enemy of man.

These temptations, though, do not have to enter into our souls. Like Our Lord, who fought the devil's suggestions with perfect force of a holy will, never considering Satan's evil proposals, we too, through penance and resilience, can grow in Christ to reach a similar point of strength.

As St. Alphonsus Liguori says, "If we wish to do good, we must act in opposition to our rebellious nature. In the beginning, it is particularly necessary to do violence to ourselves in order to root out bad habits, and to acquire habits of virtue. When good habits are once acquired, the observance of the divine law becomes easy, and even sweet."[2] We see this in the life of great Saints, whose initial conversion was followed by a period of intense mortification.

Fighting temptation and remaining in a state of grace require us to take account of our current commitment, and to make a plan to restructure our lives as needed. St. Alphonsus adds, "It is necessary then to adopt the means of salvation, and to lead a life of order and regularity. It is necessary after rising in the morning, to make the Christian acts of thanksgiving, love, oblation, and a purpose of avoiding sin, along with a prayer to Jesus and Mary that they may preserve you from sin during the day."[3]

In addition to making Mass, doing spiritual readings, praying the Rosary, and making an examination of conscience, St. Alphonsus says, "Above all, it is necessary to ask of God holy perseverance, and especially in the time of temptation, invoking then more frequently the names of Jesus and Mary as long as the temptation continues. If you're acting in this manner, you will certainly be saved; if not, you will certainly be lost."[4]

The voice of temptation is an invitation to damnation. We must see it like this. If we do, we will call upon Jesus and Mary to send down the Holy Spirit as fire to consume this invitation of the devil, and to scatter the forces of darkness with the light of His love.

---

[1] *Little Catechism*, p 99
[2] *Preparation for Death*, 317
[3] *Preparation for Death*, 323
[4] *Preparation for Death*, 324

A reminder of some essential points, from *Slaying Dragons*…

+ All mankind is subject to ordinary temptation and must do battle daily to avoid sin.
+ Recourse to the Sacraments, sacramentals, and the life of prayer is sufficient to thwart the tactics of the Enemy and endure his persistent attacks.
+ Temptation that is not initially resisted will lead to greater weakness to the devil's influence.
+ In every way, it is best to ignore the devil, whether in ordinary temptation or in extraordinary manifestations.
+ Diabolical activity beyond normal temptation is typically the result of a door being willingly opened to the diabolical, either by the individual or by another person against the individual.

Questions to consider:
- In temptations, when you remember to pray and to invoke the aids that God has given us, have you noticed that the spiritual battle of temptation becomes much more endurable, less intimidating, and less distracting?
- When temptation first emerges, do you address it as an invitation to damnation, or do you make light of it, as if it is merely an old weakness that occasionally resurfaces?
- Are there strong or recurrent temptations which you can easily see are connected to serious sins you have committed, as if they opened a door to greater spiritual trials?

_____

_____

_____

_____

_____

_____

_____

_____

_____

_____

_____

_____

Temptation

~CONSIDERATIONS~

#1. Within every temptation, many things are happening at once: your flaws and wounds and vices are stirred, your memories of sin and selfishness and fear are vulnerable to being brought into the situation, God is actively reaching out to you with some amount of grace to aid you, your Guardian Angel is attempting to instill in your mind holy resolve, and a certain number and kind of demons are trying to encourage you to sin while remaining completely hidden in the process. Sin is no small matter. Think about how this plays out with a specific sin in your life.
- How can you prepare ahead of time to respond to God's work in your soul and oppose the devil's efforts?

_____
_____
_____
_____
_____
_____
_____

#2. When enduring a strong temptation, have you considered the fact that, in addition to the teaching that God never gives us more than we can handle, the demons are restricted in how much they can tempt us? Thus, in every temptation, our ability to resist the demons, with the aid of grace, is greater than the power of their temptation against us.
- Think about a specific sin: how have you seen this battle play out? Have you seen how the temptation is only <u>so</u> strong, or that, when you ask God for help, the temptation becomes notably limited?

_____
_____
_____
_____
_____
_____
_____
_____

#3. In the spiritual war, specific demons have dedicated themselves to stirring mankind to specific sins in order to wound us and corrupt our spiritual lives, thus ensuring our damnation. Fornication, abortion, homosexual acts, pornography, adultery, and the like are key mortal sins in their plan today. Often, we arrive at these sins through a temptation toward other sins that lay at the root of these impure desires. These root sins include vanity, pride, condemnation of others, and envy.
- Given the above, how resilient are you against these specific sins, and temptations related to these?
- How resilient are you against these root sins?

#4. Demons are driven by certain principles and perspectives that do not change. As a result, you will likely see a pattern to your temptations. Search the sins that plague you and see if they tend to occur when your mind has not been readily inclined to think about God.
- When you drift from God, do your weaknesses grow?
- When you get distracted from relying on God's Providence, for example, and try to take complete control over your life, do you begin to get angry and agitated toward others?
- Do certain sins seem to flow from other sins you commit?

Temptation

#5. Once you have identified your primary temptations, search through the Bible to find verses that speak to these temptations. There are many good Bible searches online where you can search for keywords and concepts. Write them down and read over them daily, asking the Holy Spirit to impart to you the graces that He promises through His Word.[5]

___

#6. Curiosity motivated Eve to enter into a near occasion of sin as she listened to the voice of Satan. A near occasion of sin is a situation in which you know you will be tempted beyond your power to resist. Curiosity, though, can often cause us to suspend our better judgment of the danger of a situation, out of a desire for the potential good we see in the forbidden act, whatever it may be.
- In your daily routine, what are these temptations that subtly sneak into your mind and draw you toward a compromise of your better judgment?
- Can you identify what initiates this and develop a plan to avoid it?

___

[5] Biblegateway.com has been a great resource for me in my studies and research. You can find all the Catholic translations, position them side-by-side, and search for specific words and topics.

#7. Some people are simply fascinated by the stories of possessions and other manifestations of the diabolical, but it is through the ordinary everyday subtle and secret temptations that the devil snares most souls into Hell.
- Are you more alert to the everyday temptations than you are intrigued by the extraordinary manifestations of the diabolical?

#8. Occasionally, and regrettably, we may grow tired of performing the acts of devotion that express our obedience to God, such as daily prayer, at least weekly Mass, avoiding sins, going to Confession often and whenever necessary, denying ourselves certain pleasures of this world, etc. If you do, take note of the source of this weariness.
- Is it the Holy Spirit, counselling you to relax in your devotions?
- Or is it the Evil One seeking to draw you into weariness and sadness, by which he can bend your will to lukewarmness and apathy?
- Is there a sin or worldly enjoyment which is presenting itself as more beneficial to you than the devotion in question?

Temptation

#9. Have you ever considered that you were plagued by a certain temptation or weakness which, for years perhaps, you have been unable to conquer? This does not necessarily mean it is the result of a targeted temptation by a specific demon, but it could be.
- What more might you need to be doing to block and resist this temptation?
- Are you taking to proper steps to secure your spiritual life?
- If so, are you implementing the proper spiritual warfare tactics? See the *Spiritual Warfare Checklist* on page 169 as a guide to what is essential.

Name the temptation and think of all the ways it manifests, other sins it encourages, passions that it stirs, and how it overall agitates you and seeks to steal your peace. Renounce it and ask Our Lord for help.

Slaying Dragons – Prepare for Battle

~ADDITIONAL NOTES FOR THIS SECTION~

Temptation

~PRAYER~

Shine Thy light, my God,
into the dark regions of my soul,
that I may always believe and see
the means of escape Thou hast left for me.
For there is no Enemy whose assault
has not been foreseen by Thee,
and whose destruction has not been provided for.
Illuminate and fortify with the strength of Thy grace,
my will and my determination to persevere in holiness.
Amen.

X: Considering Extraordinary Phenomena

Patron Saints: St. Teresa of Avila and St. John of the Cross

~PRAYER~

I rely on Thy power,
my King and my God,
my Savior and my Redeemer,
O Prince of Peace.
I adore Thy goodness in the truths Thou hast revealed
and the warnings Thou hast provided,
should we become wayward, cowardly, or lukewarm in our love for Thee.
Defend me, O God, against a godless nation,
against the principalities and powers, against the hosts of wickedness.
Let not my feet go astray,
for there awaits a dragon, a ferocious lion, to devour my soul.
Let me not be shaken, nor permit fear to overtake me,
for this dragon will become but a dead snake underfoot
for those who abide in Thee.
Crush, then, this vile serpent, and all the agencies by which he operates.
Dispel the darkness beneath the wings of this dragon.
Repel him by Thy power and block him from tempting me any further.
May the power of Thy Holy Cross
and the purity of Thy Most Precious Blood,
shield me from the assaults of this Enemy
and refresh my soul with the streams of Thy divine mercy.
Amen.

~INTRODUCTION~

It is on account of our sins, or of the transgression of Adam, that the Lord also allows the extraordinary activity of the Devil. As in the case of the woman, "bound by Satan," whom Our Lord heals, whose body was bent over, unable to look up, so too the devil seeks to cast our glances to the earth, stealing the sight of heaven from our hearts. "For every sinner who thinks earthly things, not seeking those that are in heaven, is unable to look up," says St. Gregory.[1] But Our Lord is glorified in His mercy when, in the moments when we, in various ways, experience the oppression of the devil, He, by the extension of His hands, liberates us from our captivity.

---

[1] St. Thomas Aquinas, *Catena Aurea*, Luke 13

Slaying Dragons – Prepare for Battle

Reflections on Sacred Scripture

The following Scripture verses relate to the theme of this section. Read through them slowly, noticing what stands out in each passage. Does a verse convict you of something you are lacking? Does a verse confirm that you are being faithful, thus clearing away doubts? Does a verse strike your heart with a new understanding of God and His holy will?

~~~

~EPHESIANS 2:2-3~
Wherein in time past you walked according to the course of this world, according to the prince of the power of this air, of the spirit that now worketh on the children of unbelief: In which also we all conversed in time past, in the desires of our flesh, fulfilling the will of the flesh and of our thoughts, and were by nature children of wrath, even as the rest.

~1 JOHN 5:19~
The whole world is in the power of the evil one.

~1 JOHN 3:8~
He who commits sin is of the devil; for the devil has sinned from the beginning. The reason the Son of God appeared was to destroy the works of the devil.

~JOHN 8:34-35~
Jesus answered them, "Truly, truly, I say to you, every one who commits sin is a slave to sin. The slave does not continue in the house for ever

~JOHN 8:44~
You are of your father the devil, and your will is to do your father's desires. He was a murderer from the beginning, and has nothing to do with the truth, because there is no truth in him. When he lies, he speaks according to his own nature, for he is a liar and the father of lies.

~LUKE 8:29-30~
For he had commanded the unclean spirit to come out of the man. (For many a time it had seized him; he was kept under guard, and bound with chains and fetters, but he broke the bonds and was driven by the demon into the desert.) Jesus then asked him, "What is your name?" And he said, "Legion"; for many demons had entered him.

~ACTS 19:15-16~
But the evil spirit answered them, "Jesus I know, and Paul I know; but who are you?" And the man in whom the evil spirit was leaped on them, mastered all of them, and overpowered them, so that they fled out of that house naked and wounded.

~LUKE 13:16~
And ought not this woman, a daughter of Abraham whom Satan bound for eighteen years, be loosed from this bond on the sabbath day?

Considering Extraordinary Phenomena

~JOHN 13:2; 26-27~
And during supper, when the devil had already put it into the heart of Judas Iscariot, Simon's son, to betray him…So when he had dipped the morsel, he gave it to Judas, the son of Simon Iscariot. Then after the morsel, Satan entered into him.

~LUKE 22:53~
This is your hour, and the power of darkness.

~MATTHEW 4:2-3~
And he fasted forty days and forty nights, and afterward he was hungry. And the tempter came and said to him, "If you are the Son of God, command these stones to become loaves of bread."

~JOHN 14:30~
I will no longer talk much with you, for the ruler of this world is coming. He has no power over me.

~JOHN 12:31 DR~
Now is the judgment of the world: now shall the prince of this world be cast out.

From the Scriptures:
- Even from the mouth of Our Lord Himself, we hear of the power of the Evil One in the world.
- When we sin, we become slaves of the devil, and it is by this that he gains dominion over us.
- Demons are many and are capable of various forms of oppression, all of which Our Lord is capable of overcoming.
- The devil was given power even over Our Lord's earthly existence, and, in this war on Christ, Satan pledges to make war on all who follow Him as well.

As you begin crafting your spiritual warfare Battle Plan, take a moment to process the above verses, and where they may have convicted you regarding your awareness of the devil's activity in the world.
1. Do I keep a good balance between the belief that Satan is real and waging a war against us and that Christ has already obtained the definitive victory?
2. When I get lazy in my dedication to holiness, do I see, in my actions and desires, the truth of the teaching that sin has made me, to some extent, a slave to sin and evil desires?

_____
_____
_____
_____
_____

Slaying Dragons – Prepare for Battle

Considering Extraordinary Phenomena

~PONDERANCE~

The consideration of the power that demons have to operate in this world is frightening to many, understandably. However, the complete teaching of the Church on the matter of the work of demons provides a great clarity which can bring peace to those who are troubled.

The majority of people mistakenly acquire their understanding of the work of the diabolical from Hollywood or other secular and non-Catholic sources. This will only lead to a disordered understanding of the devil's power and inevitably lead the person into a state of fear or of doubt regarding the existence of demons.

Demons, however, are quite real. The history of divine revelation, the history of mankind, and the testimony of the Church and her exorcists gives overwhelming evidence of the presence of the diabolical. Our role and relevance with regard to these evil spirits is where the truth must be known, for demons have no other care but for robbing us of eternal life.

Our world is primed to welcome and invite diabolical activity into our lives. In God's plan, demons are capable of quite a bit of activity. However, as we know, God blocks almost all the activity in which they would like to be engaged in this world. That being said, as a result of our sinfulness, and that of the world itself, many doors are opened for them to gain permission to act against us.

As a result, we must be fortified against them. This can only happen by being faithful to Christ and His Holy Church. Without this, we are in the devil's territory. So, we must know the abilities of the demons, the means by which they may act against us, and the weapons and means by which we can repel them and shut the doors against them.

Once all of this is in place, we can navigate this world with very few disturbances. We will be able to live in peace, with no fear of the working of the diabolical. Further, should anything odd manifest in our lives, or the life of someone we know, we will be fully equipped with both knowledge and sacramentals to drive these forces of evil away.

Consider the example of St. Benedict, the patron of exorcists and the founder of Western monasticism. He knew the power of the devil and the power of prayer to thwart him. When reforming a monastery, the monks grew resentful of the austerity and tried to poison him. St. Benedict, as was his custom, made the Sign of the Cross over a pitcher of wine before the meal, in which the poison had been placed.

As St. Gregory states, "It broke at his blessing as if he had struck it with a stone… [for it] could not bear the sign of life."[2] In like manner, the grace of the Lord shatters the workings of the diabolical. The Church fully believes this as well and has enriched her sacramental blessings with such language, promising a powerful protection against all evil to those who love God.

---

[2] *The Life and Miracles of St. Benedict*, Ch. 3

A reminder of some essential points, from *Slaying Dragons*...

+ Extraordinary diabolical activities are typically rare but are all becoming more common today.
+ In these extraordinary manifestations, demons are allowed to attack the imagination of the person, the senses of the person, the person's possessions, and at times the body of the person.
+ Demons are also allowed to orchestrate external events in a manner designed to inflict harm or suffering upon the person or bring aggravations into the person's life.
+ Demons are also allowed to cause apparent illnesses. These will merely be symptoms resembling a real illness but will only be driven away by prayers.
+ Demons are capable of causing mental and physical illnesses, which are distinguished from authentically natural causes by the prayers of the exorcist.
+ Demons are able to manipulate the body of the possessed in quite startling ways during the exorcism.
+ When a priest prays over a person, if a demon is present, it will manifest in some way. Some manifestations are subtle while others are obvious.
+ The time it takes for a person to be liberated varies greatly and depends on many factors including the spiritual work done by the possessed to aid the liberation.
+ The exorcism inflicts a real pain upon the demon which, as a result, is effective in driving them out of a person's body.
+ Cases of possession are rare. Less than ten percent of people who come to see an exorcist have a true case of possession.
+ There are four classic signs that a person is possessed: aversion to the sacred, secret knowledge, fluency in unknown languages, superhuman strength.
+ It is possible for children to be possessed as a result of demons in the family line or through forced involvement of the child in Satanic rituals.
+ There are three ways by which a person may become possessed, each depending on God's permission: mortal sin, serious trauma, and by the will of God.

Questions to consider:
- Is your understanding of the abilities of demons informed primarily by the teachings of the Church and her exorcists, or by the sensational portrayals from Hollywood?
- There are real risks today, even more than in times past, of falling into the trap of the diabolical: are you taking the occult and mortal sin seriously in your life and that of your family?

___
___
___

Considering Extraordinary Phenomena

~CONSIDERATIONS~

#1. Have you ever witnessed in your home strange phenomena that had no natural explanation? Have you wondered whether or not these events were the work of a demon? The first assumption in these cases is that there is some natural explanation. However, if all natural explanations fail to explain it, don't hesitate to call your priest to bless the house and/or offer Mass in the home.

#2. In prayer, we sometimes experience the sensation of having a vision or of some other sort of strange imagery in our mind or even visibly with our eyes. While God can do this, and even our minds can do this, the demons can also do this.
- Do you remember anything that has appeared to you, even mentally, in prayer, which you are unable to forget?
- Have you ever become attached to this sensation, desiring to see these things more frequently, and trying to have some control over them?

Rest assured: if God desires to give you a vision, you will know. In the meantime, it is best to ignore them and move on. As you recall them now with clarity, see if some aspect stands out as clearly a trick of these eyes or as more clearly something else.

_____

_____

_____

_____

_____

_____

_____

#3. Demons can manifest in our lives in extraordinary ways, if God permits them. If we are living in a state of grace, the demons do not have permission to harass us except by a rare allowance of God. This is typically reserved for the greatest of Saints, who don't really mind at that point, or to those who have opened themselves up to extraordinary diabolical activity through persistent grave sin or the occult.

Remind yourself of this and then place yourself anew in the presence of the God who promises to protect you.
- Have you ever found yourself burdened by a sense of fear about these things happening to you?
- Is this fear based on any memory of involvement in grave sin or the occult, or is it disconnected from any logical explanation?

Considering Extraordinary Phenomena

#4. Some people do have strange things happen to them, such as the appearance of a shadowy figure in their room or hallway, particularly when it is dark or at night. This can leave people disturbed or simply confused. There are additional signs that will accompany these manifestations if they are diabolical. Otherwise, in the absence of those signs, it can very likely simply be a trick of the eyes. If you find yourself fearful of these things, remind yourself that these oddities likely have a natural cause.

#5. Illnesses which do not respond properly or manifest in a peculiar manner can give them impression that their origin is not natural. Curses, and diabolical activity as a result of sin, can lead to illnesses, both physical and psychological.
- If you have any peculiar medical issues that seem not to respond to medicine in the way that they should, it could be a good idea to speak to a competent priest about it to get his thoughts.
- If he agreed that something seemed off, he would talk to you about the situation and your spiritual life.
- If he thought it would be helpful, he might start with some simple deliverance prayers in order to try to gauge the possibility of diabolical involvement.
- It may simply be the case that an improvement and deepening of your spiritual life is sufficient to bring clarity and, potentially, relief from what has been burdening you.[3]

Remember, though, an illness should always be assumed to have a natural cause. It is only when additional indicators are present that it should be considered for possible diabolical involvement.

---

[3] See page 169 for the *Spiritual Warfare Checklist*

Considering Extraordinary Phenomena

~ADDITIONAL NOTES FOR THIS SECTION~

Slaying Dragons – Prepare for Battle

~PRAYER~

Shelter me, O God,
and place Thy healing balm upon me,
that the wounds and scars I bear from this life
will not hinder me in persevering in Thy grace.
Create a fortress around my heart
where Thou alone mayest reside
and from which perfect praise for Thy glory may go up.
Let Thy holy angels and Thy saints,
and Thy glorious and blessed ever-virgin Mother,
Mary Immaculate,
abide with me in this fortress
that the bangings and rattlings and calls of the Evil one,
the many efforts he makes to gain my attention,
may be drowned in the sacred melodies
echoing forth from my soul unto eternal glory.
Amen.

XI: The Effects of the Occult

Patron Saint: Bl. Bartolo Longo

~PRAYER~

Forgive me, Lord,
for the times when I have sought my happiness
or solutions to my problems
outside of Thy love and Thy laws.
Forgive me for making an idol
of my anger, of my sadness,
of food and other pleasures,
instead of orienting my life around Thy goodness.
Break me free, O Divine Master,
from any evil attachments and shackles which I have created
by turning to creatures for my hope and my peace
instead of to Thee, my God and Creator.
Amen.

~INTRODUCTION~

An exorcist once recounted a fascinating story about a Ouija board. A young man, quite popular among his peers, played with his Ouija board with a group of friends. A spirit became present and they eventually asked the spirit to tap them on the shoulder. Instead, the spirit beat them all up so badly that the boy left the board and ran home in terror. After spending some time scared and crying on his bed, he rose and entered his bathroom. There, on the sink, was the Ouija board he had left behind, set up and ready to go.[1]

In my own work, I have heard numerous stories from youth and adults about occult activity and the response from the diabolical. Further, families are being torn apart, even those who are centered on Christ and His Church, as the diabolical, through occult curiosity, tear them apart. Youth, immersed in a Godless world, turn to the occult out of curiosity or a desire for thrills or power.

Their inability to recognize and diagnose the spiritual sicknesses that arise from the occult is one reason why the naïve, the foolish, and the ignorant continue to explore this realm. Exorcists, though, see it all the time. This is why their testimonies are so important. They all say – stay away from the occult.

---

[1] Fr. Cliff Ermatinger, *The Trouble with Magic,* Padre Pio Press, 2021, pg. 30

Reflections on Sacred Scripture
The following Scripture verses relate to the theme of this section. Read through them slowly, noticing what stands out in each passage. Does a verse convict you of something you are lacking? Does a verse confirm that you are being faithful, thus clearing away doubts? Does a verse strike your heart with a new understanding of God and His holy will?

~~~

~2 THESSALONIANS 2:9-10~
The coming of the lawless one by the activity of Satan will be with all power and with pretended signs and wonders, and with all wicked deception for those who are to perish, because they refused to love the truth and so be saved.

~REVELATION 16:13-14~
And I saw, issuing from the mouth of the dragon and from the mouth of the beast and from the mouth of the false prophet, three foul spirits like frogs; for they are demonic spirits, performing signs, who go abroad to the kings of the whole world, to assemble them for battle on the great day of God the Almighty.

~REVELATION 22:14-15~
Blessed are those who wash their robes, that they may have the right to the tree of life and that they may enter the city by the gates. Outside are the dogs and sorcerers and fornicators and murderers and idolaters, and every one who loves and practices falsehood.

~REVELATION 21:7-8~
He who conquers shall have this heritage, and I will be his God and he shall be my son. But as for the cowardly, the faithless, the polluted, as for murderers, fornicators, sorcerers, idolaters, and all liars, their lot shall be in the lake that burns with fire and brimstone, which is the second death.

~DEUTERONOMY 18:9-12~
When you come into the land which the LORD your God gives you, you shall not learn to follow the abominable practices of those nations. There shall not be found among you any one who burns his son or his daughter as an offering, any one who practices divination, a soothsayer, or an augur, or a sorcerer, or a charmer, or a medium, or a wizard, or a necromancer. For whoever does these things is an abomination to the LORD; and because of these abominable practices the LORD your God is driving them out before you.

~EZEKIEL 13:18, 20~
And say, Thus says the Lord GOD: Woe to the women who sew magic bands upon all wrists, and make veils for the heads of persons of every stature, in the hunt for souls! Will you hunt down souls belonging to my people, and keep other souls alive for your profit? Wherefore thus says the Lord GOD: Behold, I am against your magic bands with which you hunt the souls, and I will tear them from your arms; and I will let the souls that you hunt go free like birds.

The Effects of the Occult

~ACTS 19:18-19~
Many also of those who were now believers came, confessing and divulging their practices. And a number of those who practiced magic arts brought their books together and burned them in the sight of all.

~ACTS 13:9-12~
But El'ymas the magician (for that is the meaning of his name) withstood them, seeking to turn away the proconsul from the faith. But Saul, who is also called Paul, filled with the Holy Spirit, looked intently at him and said, "You son of the devil, you enemy of all righteousness, full of all deceit and villainy, will you not stop making crooked the straight paths of the Lord? And now, behold, the hand of the Lord is upon you, and you shall be blind and unable to see the sun for a time." Immediately mist and darkness fell upon him and he went about seeking people to lead him by the hand. Then the proconsul believed.

~2 TIMOTHY 2:25-26~
God may perhaps grant that they will repent and come to know the truth, and they may escape from the snare of the devil, after being captured by him to do his will.

From the Scriptures:
- The condemnation of magic and sorcery and idolatry could not be clearer in Sacred Scripture.
- Demonic spirits have the power to perform pretended signs and wonders in this world, but their intention is to deceive mankind and ensure that they perish.
- When God encounters the activity of witchcraft and magic, He issues the strongest warnings and condemnations, and promises that His power will eradicate the effects of these spells.
- As the Gospel moved through the world in the early Church, it came with power and conviction against the idolatry of magic, freeing souls from its snares.
- When we engage the world of darkness, whether by habitual mortal sin or forms of witchcraft, we become slaves to Satan, captured by him and doing his will.

As you begin crafting your spiritual warfare Battle Plan, take a moment to process the above verses, and where they may have convicted you regarding the importance of avoiding the occult.
1. Have you, or ones you loved, been open to witchcraft or other forms of magic, and have you prayed appropriately to obtain, for yourself of another, freedom from these snares?
2. Have you ever been convinced of the power of the occult or another false religion by the manifestations that have emerged from occultic rituals that rely on the power of demons?
3. If you have practiced magic in the past, do you fully understand and embrace the power of the Gospel and grace to free you completely from it?

Slaying Dragons – Prepare for Battle

The Effects of the Occult

~PONDERANCE~

Exorcists observe the true reality of the evil of dabbling in the occult. It is not a matter of childhood fascination or curious exploration. Dabbling in the occult, even once, brings the person face-to-face with the diabolical. It is up to God as to whether or not a demon is permitted to engage with the person as a result of that activity.

However, again, exorcists see far too many cases where the extraordinary diabolical activity in a person's life began with a single dabbling in the occult, like visiting a palm reader, or what a teenager may think is an "innocent game." An evil attachment can be formed in just that one instance since that activity is a mortal sin and an act of idolatry. Cases of possession have been known to have begun with one open door to the occult such as this.

Demons are real and they occupy more of our world than secularized people want to admit. Despite that incredulity, the demons will take advantage of anything we offer them. They are opportunists. Very often, they lure people away from God by suggesting to them realms of "immediate answers" and "immediate gratification." We must trust God, turn to Him, and abide by His timeline.

The effects of the occult can appear in the same day or week as the sin, or they can manifest years later. Any fraternizing with something in the modern category of "occult" must be renounced, rejected, and taken to Confession. Exorcists have heard demons confess that a case of possession, for a man in his thirties, actually began when he dabbled in the occult as a teenager. The diabolical entanglement does not always manifest; sometimes it has to be provoked to know it is there.

Stories abound, as recounted in *Slaying Dragons*, of the power of shrines and pilgrimages and Saints to draw the diabolical to the surface, so the Church can then cast it out. Sometimes, the mere presence of a Saint, such as St. John Bosco or St. Catherine of Sienna, is sufficient to send the demon into a mad sprint in the other direction, never to molest the person again.

The occult encompasses a wide range of activities, all originating from a superstitious or magical mindset. This mindset, which sets us or created things as sources of power, turns us into idolators. In this, we make the demon into a god, and, through our occult practice, bind ourselves to that evil spirit, which, regardless of whether possession occurs, ends up placing us in a "demonic enslavement of the soul."[2]

With the occult on the rise, and many children and young people falling prey to it, all the faithful need to understand the seriousness of its effects.

---

[2] Fr. Bamonte, *Diabolical Possession and the Ministry of Exorcism*, Pope Leo XIII Institute Press, 2014, pg. 39

Slaying Dragons – Prepare for Battle

A reminder of some essential points, from *Slaying Dragons*…

+ We must stay away from things that are affiliated with the diabolical and not let curiosity lead us to test the spiritual realm.
+ The occult and Satanic groups in the world are aware of the networking of exorcists and seek to infiltrate it to learn what exorcists know.
+ The statistics regarding the rise in consultation with the occult across the globe are startling.
+ Popular culture and society have become very open and curious about mystical, occultic, and diabolical things, which presents a grave danger, particularly to the youth.
+ Satanism is now in a position where it feels welcomed and entitled to its share of public space and the public forum.
+ The number and variety of New Age practices are also on the increase and pose a serious threat to those in spiritually vulnerable situations.
+ Popular practices, like Yoga and Reiki, popular literature, like *Harry Potter*, and popular entertainment, like many shows on *Disney,* are clear examples of how entrenched the occult has become in modern society.
+ Some people choose to make pacts with the devil. While the devil is a liar, he often still gives what was promised, but completely destroys the person's life in the process, in a strategic way designed to lead them to damnation.

Questions to consider:
- Do you pray often for those who are involved in the occult, particularly the youth?
- When you seek to be entertained by this post-Christian society, do you prudently navigate the choices offered to you so you do not allow yourself to be exposed to a slow immersion in the occult?
- Are you aware that those who do not resolve situations where they are tempted by such things as a spirit of revenge, or seek knowledge about others which is secret, are vulnerable to the devil's tempting them further into direct contact with the occult?

The Effects of the Occult

~CONSIDERATIONS~

#1. Recourse to the occult places the person in a state of sinning against the First Commandment and highly likely brings them into the presence of a demon.
- Have you ever made a pact with a demon, summoned a spirit, or desired to receive power or revenge so much that you were even open to receiving it from the devil himself, should he have offered it to you?
- Have you ever sought out a psychic, fortune teller, palm reader, or medium in order to find a solution to a problem that burdened you or make contact with a deceased loved one?
    - o If so, think carefully about that act. Recall the story to yourself, especially if the memory is foggy, and take it to your priest in Confession. Depending on the details, you may need to speak with him outside of Confession as well, to be certain it is dealt with properly.
    - o Also, look at the *Renunciation of Evil Actions and Influences* on page 175 and *Binding Prayers* on page 183, for prayers to use to renounce this association and bind any demons who may be plaguing you.

_____
_____
_____
_____
_____
_____
_____

#2. Think carefully about all the items in your home, things you have collected over the years or decades, things given to you as antiques from your family, or things you have recently acquired. Is there anything that is of questionable origin or artwork or intention? If so, take a look again, do some research, and follow up if you have any concerns. If all seems well, be at peace. If something is of the occult or suspicious, see *What to Do with Occult and Cursed Items*, on page 173 for how to properly destroy an occult item.
- Make a list of the items in the space below if helpful.

_____
_____

#3. Generational spirits can enter a family through grave sins such as the occult. Do some research on your family to see if any recent generations have been involved in such things. If they were, you will need to renounce these sins and discard or destroy any items that they may have passed down to you that are related to these sins or the occult. See *What to Do with Occult and Cursed Items,* for how to properly destroy an occult item.
- Depending on what it is, it might be helpful to speak to your priest about it as well.
- If it is related to Freemasonry, see the *Protocol for Praying to Break the Freemasonic Curse,* on page 179, for how to break the Freemasonic curse, if that applies to you.
- If you do not discover anything, then entrust your family history to Our Lord and be at peace.

#4. Curses are real, unfortunately, and their power, which is diabolical, can influence innocent people. One of the common causes of curses and diabolical influence is Freemasonry.
- Has there been a Freemason in your family in recent generations? If so, this needs to be resolved. See the *Protocol for Praying to Break the Freemasonic Curse,* on page 179, for details about the Freemasonic curse.

The Effects of the Occult

~ADDITIONAL NOTES FOR THIS SECTION~

Slaying Dragons – Prepare for Battle

~PRAYER~

Protect my heart, Lord Jesus,
for in it are many wounds.
I know the Evil One seeks to corrupt me there,
to fill me with despair and pride,
to elevate something disordered within me
into an idol that replaces Thee.
I renew my gift, my heart to Thee.
I bind myself to Thee, O Lord,
who first bound Thyself to me in Baptism.
I am all Thine, and all that I have belongs to Thee,
O my sweet Jesus,
through Mary, Thy holy Mother.
Amen.

XII: The Ministry of the Exorcist

Patron Saint: Servant of God, Fr. Candido Amantini

We are not alone in this world. This truth applies not just to the laity but also to the great priests and exorcists who hand on to us the sacred and saving Truths of our Holy Faith.

As all know who have read this book and *Slaying Dragons*, we are in debt to exorcists and to the great priests who labor to teach us and instruct us in the rich traditions of the Church. As a result, we need to appreciate what they do for us and do all we can to support them.

The ministry of exorcism is at the core of the message and mission of Christ and His Church. It is important to understand this, as it places the work of modern exorcists in the context of the central mission of the Messiah.

The following verses of Sacred Scripture depict the presence and centrality of this ministry:

#1. Our Lord Himself is the chief Exorcist. One of His primary works was to deliver mankind from bondage to the Devil:

~MATTHEW 14:17-18~
"Bring him here to me." And Jesus rebuked him, and the demon came out of him, and the boy was cured instantly.

~~~

#2. The work of exorcism is a command of Our Lord. Though it is not a Sacrament, it is listed as one of the powers that comes with the office of Apostle:

~MATTHEW 10:1~
And he called to him his twelve disciples and gave them authority over unclean spirits, to cast them out, and to heal every disease and every infirmity.

~~~

#3. With the authority given to them by Christ, the demons responded to the seventy men chosen by Our Lord as to ones who had authority over them:

~LUKE 10:17-20~
The seventy returned with joy, saying, "Lord, even the demons are subject to us in your name!" And he said to them, "I saw Satan fall like lightning from heaven. Behold, I have given you authority to tread upon serpents and scorpions, and over all the power of the enemy; and nothing shall hurt you. Nevertheless do not rejoice in this, that the spirits are subject to you; but rejoice that your names are written in heaven."

~~~

#4. In the ministry of Paul and the Apostles, we see in the Acts of the Apostles their power over evil spirits and their ability to authoritatively drive them out of people:

~ACTS 16:16-18~

As we were going to the place of prayer, we were met by a slave girl who had a spirit of divination and brought her owners much gain by soothsaying. She followed Paul and us, crying, "These men are servants of the Most High God, who proclaim to you the way of salvation." And this she did for many days. But Paul was annoyed, and turned and said to the spirit, "I charge you in the name of Jesus Christ to come out of her." And it came out that very hour.

~~~

A reminder of some essential points, from *Slaying Dragons*...

+ What exorcists see in their ministry is in harmony with what Sacred Scripture and the Church teach to be true.
+ Exorcists depend on a network of support for their ministries. Seminaries are inadequately preparing priests for this ministry and newly appointed exorcists often struggle to acquire what they need in order to be formed well.
+ The best way to train an exorcist is for him to witness the reality with his own eyes.
+ Exorcists learn a great deal about their ministry and the work of demons by attending conferences with other exorcists and by hearing stories from what actually happens inside exorcisms.
+ Exorcists are studying whether the souls of the damned are capable of possessing people, as a result of certain phenomena observed in exorcisms.
+ Medical and diabolical issues often overlap, and it is important for exorcists to have some background or familiarity with psychology to better navigate the ambiguities of some of the symptoms.
+ Exorcists look for certain signs and phenomena which indicate that a mental or physical illness is actually diabolical in origin.
+ Exorcists depend on the support of a team of devout Catholics to assist them at exorcisms.
+ The liberation is a slow process that requires forcing the demon to communicate and acquiring the information necessary to gain control over the demon.
+ There are many sacred traditions in our Faith of which people are, more or less, unaware today but which exorcists see and teach to be valuable sources of spiritual strength.

The Ministry of the Exorcist

~PRAYING FOR OUR EXORCISTS~

Based on the above, and on what we have learned in *Slaying Dragons* about the difficulties modern exorcists face, it is important that we pray for them, and for their specific needs. Take a moment and read through these suggestions, and offer prayers such as these daily for our exorcists:

+ Pray for exorcists to have the gift of understanding that they might discern the true power of the Sacraments and sacramentals entrusted to them by the Church to aid their ministry of healing and liberation.

+ Pray for exorcists to have the gift of wisdom that they may be able to detect the root of what troubles the individuals whom they seek to help with their authority, that they may be able to guide the afflicted along the proper course to healing.

+ Pray for exorcists to be strong men, able to endure the viciousness of demons and the cruelty with which they manifest in the lives of the possessed.

+ Pray that exorcists, particularly those newly appointed, will find the support of both experienced exorcists and lay faithful who will commit to assisting them by their prayers.

+ Pray that exorcists will have access to the intellectual resources necessary to grow and be grounded in their ministry, such as books, wise mentors, and conferences designed to guide them and answer their questions.

+ Pray that exorcists can correctly discern what is true and what is false in their interactions with the diabolical in the course of the exorcisms.

+ Pray that the Holy Spirit will impart His gifts and charisms to exorcists and the lay faithful that, together, as a team, the exorcist and his assistants may aid, by their holiness, the liberation of the afflicted souls who seek their help.

Slaying Dragons – Prepare for Battle

~Prayer~

Almighty God,
Thou hast revealed Thy power over evil
in the Incarnation of Thine only-begotten Son, Our Lord Jesus Christ.
In His ministry in the Gospels,
in His consistent victory over the work of the diabolical,
He showed us that He holds all authority in heaven and on earth.
In His supreme goodness,
He has continued this great victory through the ministry of His priests,
and in particular His chosen co-workers who seek the liberation of souls from the snares of Satan.
We ask Thee, O bountiful Lord,
to bestow upon these exorcists, and upon all priests who collaborate in this ministry,
special graces of fortitude, prudence, humility, charity, hope,
and surrender to Thy Providence.
Uproot from their souls any stains of sin
which they may have incurred in the years in which they have walked through this valley of tears.
Illuminate their intellects and strengthen their wills
that, as champions of faith, they may,
by believing,
wield the full power of Your grace.
May these graces quicken their steps along the path of perfection
and make mighty their voices against the agents of darkness.
Mary Immaculate, Undoer of Knots and Mother of Sorrows,
defend them in their battle against the forces of evil.
Stay by their side and guarantee that,
through the faithful exercise of their office,
the wickedness of our Adversary may be subdued, his rage silenced, and his power thwarted.
May all who invoke or hear the Holy Names of Jesus and Mary
experience the comfort of their power
and find the freedom promised to the sons of God.
Amen.

Part II

Prayers, Reflections, & Resources for Spiritual Purification & Renewal

Spiritual Warfare Checklist

When we have spiritual struggles, especially ones that are unusual or burdensome, in order to begin the process of finding relief and strength, we must analyze the state of our soul and our practice of the Faith. There are many fundamental things which must be considered first, before proceeding to others. Often, the burden or struggle can be addressed by a renewal of the fundamental structures of grace in our souls, which then restores the source of divine life or increases its flow into our souls.

After this, if we are still burdened by the wounds from our sins or are not progressing in the way we would like, we must consider how well we are taking up the spiritual arms provided by the Church. These weapons are critical for any person who desires to both make and maintain spiritual progress. The basics of spiritual warfare will bring noticeable strength and clarity to our souls and produce many of the spiritual effects that we desire.

Still, for many people, they realize that, despite ensuring that the foundations of grace and spiritual warfare are in place, they still feel stunted in their spiritual growth or burdened by excessive temptations, worries, or other spiritual concerns. At this point, the Church provides a more advanced treatment to the soul and weightier spiritual weapons. These are not necessary for everyone and are primarily utilized by those who have suffered from serious sin or a life of sin, the effects of the occult, or family involvement in Freemasonry or other malevolent practices.

First things for each person to consider:
- Am I in a state of grace?
- If married, was I married in the Church and according to the Church's laws?
- Does my family live in accordance with the authority structure that God has willed for it?
- Have I been to Confession in the last month?
- Do I go to Holy Mass every Sunday and receive Holy Communion?
- Do I set aside Sunday as a Holy Day and keep it in honor of Our Lord?
- Do I completely adhere to the teachings of the Church or have I modified those teachings to suit my own desires?
- Do I pray every day, ideally at least fifteen minutes?
- Do I fast and abstain from meat regularly as a penance and source of grace?
- Do I pray the Holy Rosary every day?
- Do I seek to avoid all sin every day and ask for forgiveness when I fall?
- Do I keep track of my sins and take them all, mortal and venial, to Confession?
- Do I seek to avoid over-indulgence of any created good?
- Do I seek to enjoy proper leisure activities to give myself necessary rest?
- Do I avoid gossip and strive to always think well of others?
- Do I seek to be humble?
- Do I avoid permissiveness toward the sins of others and seek to lead others to holiness?

Slaying Dragons – Prepare for Battle

The next things to consider:
- Are there any items in my house (books, videos, images) that promote vice, sinful curiosity, immodesty, or promiscuity?
- Do I tolerate television or video programs that subtly suggest or present immoral images, innuendo, lifestyles, or suggestions?
- Do I avoid pornography, abortion, contraception, adultery, and any other major mortal sins?
- Have I had my house and my car blessed by a priest?
- Do I bless my home with holy water or blessed salt periodically?[1]
- Do I bless my children regularly?
- Do I have additional sacramentals in the house, like blessed candles, blessed Crucifixes on the walls, and sacred images of Our Lord, Our Lady, and the Angels and Saints?[2]
- Do I wear a Scapular and abide by the promises it entails?
- Do I wear a St. Benedict medal?
- Do I try to fulfill the First Friday and First Saturday devotions?
- Do I go to Confession every two weeks and whenever I am in need or I sense that going to Confession would help in dealing with a strong temptation?
- Do I go to Daily Mass every time I am able?
- Do I seek to fill my mind with sacred thoughts, imagery, and sounds, in order to sanctify myself and drive out any diabolical activity?
- Did I pick up any deep wounds to my soul in the years of my past when I lived in sin?
- Have I sought to acquire spiritual healing for all of the moral wounds I may have suffered in my past?
- Do I use the binding prayer against all, and especially persistent, temptations toward sin?

Finally:
- Do I regularly do anything that exposes me to diabolical activity or influences?
- Are there any items that are tied to the occult in my house?
- Have I renounced any connections I may have had in the past to the occult?
- Have I dabbled in the occult in the past and not brought that up in Confession?
- Have I renounced all of the major mortal sins, like habitual sins against the flesh, fornication, abortion, adultery, pornography, and the occult, that I have ever committed in my life?
- Did I ever allow myself to remain in a state of mortal sin without seeking Confession as soon as possible?
- If I have any connections to the Freemasons in my family, have I analyzed that to discover if I need to break any Freemasonic curses or associated curses?
- Are there any indicators that my home might be infested with a demon?
- Do I know who lived in my home prior to me?
- Are there any people living near me who practice witchcraft or other forms of the occult?
- Do I have any thoughts that are persistent, disordered, despairing, and seemingly beyond my own choosing?

---

[1] This simply involves walking through the house and sprinkling holy water or blessed salt in all the rooms. It does not need to make contact with every item in the room.

[2] It is vital that sacramentals be used with faith, reverence, and devotion, treating them as gifts from God whose power it is which makes them spiritually beneficial to us.

Spiritual Warfare Checklist

If, by the end of this checklist, you have some serious concerns remaining, it is advisable to speak to your pastor or a priest whom you trust. He might decide that another blessing of the home is in order. He might suggest practical ways to increase your personal spiritual life, including making a general Confession. He can also lead you through any renunciations of attachments to sin and, if applicable, spiritual issues related to personal or family involvement in Freemasonry. Never fear asking your pastor for help. He, or another priest, has the power and authority to lead you to God.

What to Do with Occult and Cursed Items

Occult items must be dealt with carefully. When a person realizes that an occult item is in his possession in whatever form, it is important that the item be removed or destroyed. Not all occult items are cursed. If the item is cursed, and if God permits the curse to manifest, there will be some sort of disturbance which gives an indication of this.

Even if an occult item is not cursed, it still must not be kept in the person's possession. Occult items can be idols, wicca or witchcraft symbols, Satanic symbols, any item from a witchcraft store, books on spells, Freemasonic paraphernalia, and even images associated with a musical group, as many are involved in the occult and Satanism.

While occult items are often cursed, not all cursed items are those from the occult. A curse may be placed on any item, but this fact should not cause us alarm. We should only suspect an item to be cursed if there are preternatural manifestations where it is present. That being said, priests who are knowledgeable of the current spiritual state of the world are quick to bless everything they use or consume, due to the possibility that some malevolent intention was once directed against it.

If there is the thought that an item might be cursed, or if a person has an occult item in his possession which could not first be returned to the owner, the item should be destroyed. When reading the below instructions, the strongest caution should be taken if the item is known, or suspected to be, cursed.

The item, once recognized as cursed, should not be touched directly. A cloth or a glove should be used to handle the object. If the person does touch the object, he should rinse his hands with holy water.[1] The object should then be sprinkled with holy water.

It is very important that the form of the object then be destroyed. If the object can be burned, it should be burned. If it is glass and it can be shattered, that should be done. If it can be torn into pieces, that should be done. If it is made of metal, try to break it in half or destroy it with a hammer. If it cannot be destroyed, it is recommended to tie a blessed palm branch or a St. Benedict medal to it.

Once the form is destroyed in the best way possible, the object should be buried, with a St. Benedict medal, and then sprinkled with holy water. If the item was able to be burned, the ashes should be scattered into a running stream or river.

In the process of destroying the item in this manner, the person should be praying. These prayers could include the Our Father, the Hail Mary, and the Glory Be, as well as asking Our Lord to break

---

[1] Not so much that it is poured out everywhere, but enough to cover the hands with the water containing the blessing.

any curse that may have been on the object. If the person had any ties to the occult or to the object, he should pray that Our Lord break any ties he has made to the occult or to the curse that was placed on the object. The person should also renounce any involvement in the occult, if that applies.[2]

The prayer, *Consecration of One's Exterior Goods to the Blessed Virgin Mary*, would be recommended to be said at this point as well, since the item in question was residing in the person's possession.[3]

For more information and recommended prayers, please visit the St. Michael Center for Spiritual Renewal and click on the "Prayers" tab, where there are a lot of deliverance prayers for both priests and the laity, including prayers for disposing of cursed objects.[4]

~~~

The following prayer can be used to bless any item that enters the house, and also any item that appears to be cursed, prior to destroying the form of the item.

Prayer for Blessing of an Item[5]
To bless items prior to bringing them into the home, such as item bought from a garage sale, large chain stores, etc.

"I, _____. as head of the household, command any and all evil attached or present to this (name item) to be banished, cast away and no longer affect this (name item).
(sprinkle #1) In the name of the Father,
(sprinkle #2) and of the Son,
(sprinkle #3) and of the Holy Spirit."

Then, if the item had any evil influence, break, burn and bury the item.

---

[2] Some details taken from *Disposing of Cursed Objects* from the Archdiocese of Manila Office of Exorcism (online).
[3] See page 185 for this prayer.
[4] https://www.catholicexorcism.org/deliverance-prayers-for-the-laity
[5] From the *Five Stones to Freedom Prayer Card,* by Liber Christo. Used with permission.

Renunciation of Evil Actions and Influences

The following are prayers that may be used by individuals to break ties and associations with, or repel and bind, demons that one may have become affiliated with through sin or the occult.

Spirit and Lies:

"In the Name of Jesus Christ, I rebuke, renounce and reject the spirit of _____"
"In the Name of Jesus Christ, I rebuke, renounce and reject the lie that _____."

Unholy Alliances:

"In the Name of Jesus Christ, I give back anything I took from _____ and I take back anything I gave to _____ and hereby break any and all unholy soul tie(s) with _____."

Occult:

"In the Name of Jesus Christ, I renounce the/any spirit that came to me when......... "In the Name of Jesus Christ, I renounce the spirit that operated in (e.g., the fortune teller, etc.) and I take back the authority or power that I gave to _____ (object or name)."

Command

"In the Name of Jesus Christ and by His Sovereignty in me, I command these evil spirits to be gone, and I ask the Blessed Mother to come and exercise her dominion over all angelic beings, glorified and fallen"

*Source for the above prayers.[1]

With the above, it is very helpful to consider all of the hurts, disappointments, resentments, and wounds from your life and forgive anyone who has caused these and toward whom you still hold a certain bitterness and lack of forgiveness.

---

[1] From the *Five Stones to Freedom Prayer Card*, by Liber Christo. Used with permission.

An Interior Healing Process

The following process for spiritual healing was devised by a group of exorcists who, with devout laity, discerned that this would be beneficial to souls. There are many positive reports from individuals who took this approach. It is a good way to initiate a process of healing and to gain strength and momentum in the ongoing spiritual purification process which characterizes our earthly existence.[1]

For this process, the person will need the assistance of his pastor, even if only for the first part. Before beginning the process, it would be best to explain it to the priest so he is ready to help.

Interior Healing Process

The First Part:
These first three days are done in a Church after Mass or a Holy Hour:

First Day: Write a letter to the Lord about your life: everything you remember about your life since you were little; no happy moments; ONLY struggles, difficulties, traumas, major events that wounded you and that you still remember with pain.

Second Day: Bring your letter with you. After Mass or the Holy Hour, read aloud the letter to the Lord, just as you would read it to someone sitting next to you. This would be done privately, not audibly for others to hear.

Third Day: Place the letter in an envelope, seal it, write on it "To Burn," and give it to the priest who is helping you in this process. He won't read the letter. He will just burn it for you.

On these first days, you are doing the following: **Acknowledging, Delivering, and Freeing:**

Acknowledging: All the wounds, traumas and difficulties of your life.
- You are bringing out of the "closet" things from your past that you wanted to forget but were unable to forget.
- On the first day, accompanied by the Lord, you are facing the reality of your entire life.
- On the second day, you are doing two things:
    - First, if you ever said things like: "The Lord never listened to me," "He forgot about me," "He left me alone," or "Where were You when this happened to me?", you now have the opportunity to sit in front of the Blessed Sacrament and tell Him everything about your life. That moment is going to be just for you and the Lord.

---

[1] This author was led through this Interior Healing Process just before discovering the teachings of exorcists and beginning my study which led to the writing of *Slaying Dragons*. I personally attribute great efficacy to this process.

Delivering: Secondly, by reading the letter, you are "delivering" your life to the Lord.
- On the third day, you are telling the Lord how hard you tried for so long to fix your life, to heal your wounds, to be better, but just couldn't do it right; and now you want Him to take care of everything.

Freeing: You are "freeing" yourself from the burdens of your past by offering them freely to the Lord.

Fourth and last day of the first part of the process:
Pray the Rosary and ask Our Lady to wrap you in her mantle. This day you will be praying regarding the **nine months** you were in your mother's womb, from the moment of your conception until the day you were born.

The Second Part: From this day on you will be praying the Rosary every day for each year of your life. You will be asking Our Lord and Our Blessed Mother to heal you from anything that might have happened to you during those years. The Rosary should be prayed separately from your family or daily rosary and the intention will <u>only</u> be for the healing of that particular year that you are praying about.
- For example, if you are 30 years old, you will be praying the Rosary for 30 days after completing the first four days. In total, your healing process will then take 34 days.

<u>Nine days prior to ending your process</u>, add the *Novena to Our Lady Undoer of Knots* and contact the priest assisting you in this process to schedule a day for the final "healing & deliverance prayers."

Please note that it is possible that you may get sick when praying for those years that were more difficult or traumatic. Do not be anxious. Just go to Mass, receive Communion and continue with your prayers.

It is not recommended that an individual initiates this healing process without the aid of a priest trained in deliverance prayers. Prayers at the end of the process, with the priest, involve the renunciation of past sins and evil associations, forgiveness of those who have caused harm to the individual or otherwise are needed to be forgiven, and certain deliverance prayers related to these issues in the person's life.

Protocol for Praying to Break the Freemasonic Curse

*Please read these **instructions carefully** if you are concerned about Freemasonry in your family. As exorcists have learned, the diabolical world is very legalistic. Therefore, the Freemasonic curse only applies to families in the manner described below.*

Protocol for Praying to Break the Freemasonic Curse[1]

Who needs to say these prayers of renunciation?

The Freemasonry curse passes away after the 4th generation if the curse is not affirmed. Common ways a curse is affirmed include abortion, contraception, fornication, rape, especially involving virginity. The demon sees all of these as blood and human sacrifice.

Do not use these prayers as a precautionary measure "just in case" there is any unknown or unconfirmed freemasonic membership in the family line. These prayers are only to be prayed when there is a religious context involved. This is compared to a peanut allergy in that the allergy can lay dormant and unknown until one is exposed to peanuts. In other words, once a person moves toward a true relationship with the Catholic Church the penalties invoked may appear.

Typical events that trigger FM retaliation:
- Pursuit of vocation within sacramental construct (religious life, ordination, matrimony)
- Minor children approaching sacraments of Baptism, Holy Communion, or Confirmation
- Adult conversion to Catholicism

PRAYERS FOLLOW THE BLOODLINE

In the case of a descendant whose father, grandfather and or earlier generation of grandfathers were practicing members of freemasonry, the oldest living patriarch should pray the prayers for the family line. Should this oldest living patriarch be unwilling or unable to pray these prayers then the next oldest son could do so. In the event that there is no living patriarch, then the oldest living daughter can pray these prayers. Note, that the male spouse of a descendant daughter would not have the authority to pray the prayers on behalf of his wife and her family. In kind, a woman would not have the authority to pray these prayers on behalf of her husband and his family line. Again, the prayers follow the blood through the male line.

When determining the bloodline, consider this in the same way as a legal claim to inheritance. Example: If a man (being the FM member) were to die without a will, who would be his "blood"

---

[1] By Fr. Chad Ripperger. Used with permission.

descendant to inherit his estate? First, the living sons and daughters, (not stepchildren), then, the grandchildren would be the order for inheritance. If all sons and daughters of the FM father or grandfather were deceased, it would be the living grandson or granddaughter who would pray the renunciation prayers.

HOW TO ENGAGE IN PRAYING THE PRAYERS:

The prayers can be found in Appendix III at the back of the prayer book "Deliverance Prayers for Use by the Laity." To obtain your copy go to the "shop" at www.liberchristo.org.[2] It is advisable to read through the prayers first so you know what is involved so to affirm your resolve to renounce and break the oaths involved.

ACTIVE OR PAST MEMBER of a Masonic or secret organization must pray the prayers in a sacred space (church, chapel,) in the presence of a deacon or priest. The original FM oaths were taken in an institutional setting (FM Lodge) in front of members and hierarchy. Therefore, a renunciation must follow in like manner with a Catholic institutional presence and authoritative response in the following manner:

1. To be prayed once a week for a total of three weeks (Rare exception would be that the prayers be prayed over a course of 5 days with one day between each prayer session.)
2. It is strongly advised for the efficacy of your prayers, that all those in attendance are "in" and sustain "a state of grace" during this entire protocol. One should confess any involvement in freemasonry or other secret society/fraternity prior to the sessions. If you are married, your spouse should also be present during these prayer sessions.
3. A witness should be advised to take note of any resistance or affects the person may experience or display while praying these prayers and report these to the priest or deacon on the third week. As well, the witness should have holy water available to offer the person praying the prayers so they can bless themselves should any affliction develop in response to the prayer.
4. At the end of each session the priest or deacon has specific prayers to pray while laying their stole on the client's head. These prayers are not found in the book for the laity. They are as follows:

Priest or Deacon Prayers:

The descendant says the following three times, as the priest or deacon places the stole on the client's head:

"In the name of Jesus Christ, I break the power of everything that I have renounced, and I command it to leave me now and go straight to the foot of Jesus to do with as He desires. Amen."

---

[2] Also at http://sensustraditionis.org/press/book-author/fr-chad-ripperger/ and on Amazon.

Protocol for Praying to Break the Freemasonic Curse

The priest or deacon then says three times:

"In the name of Jesus Christ, I break the power of everything that ___ has renounced, and I command it to leave him/her now and go straight to the foot of the Cross for Jesus to do with as He desires."

The priest or deacon now asks the Holy Spirit for an infilling of grace into the person.

<u>NON-MEMBER BUT DESCENDANT</u>: If you never participated in any Masonic organization but you are a descendant of someone who was, it is recommended that the appropriate member in the family blood line pray these prayers as stated above with the only exception being: The prayers are not required to be recited in the presence of a deacon or priest.

Binding Prayers

In the Name of Jesus, I bind you, spirit of _____ and I cast you to the foot of the Cross to be judged by Our Lord. Amen.

In the Name of Jesus, I renounce _____, and all the times I have embraced it, and I choose obedience to Jesus Christ and His Gospel.

Binding prayers regarding a child
I
In the Name of Jesus, I command you, spirit of _____, to depart from N. and leave him/her in peace, and I bind you and cast you to the foot of the Cross to be judged by Our Lord.

II
Jesus, I ask you to bind any evil spirits sending bad friends into N.'s life (or keeping the child friends with bad people) (or interfering in their friendships), and to send them to the Cross to receive their sentence.

Another form of Binding Prayer[1]
Spirit of N., I bind you in the Name of Jesus, by the power of the most Precious Blood of Our Lord Jesus Christ and by the intercession of the Blessed Virgin Mary, St. Michael the Archangel, the blessed Apostles Peter and Paul and all of the saints, and I command you to leave N. (name of person or object) and go to the foot of the Holy Cross to receive your sentence, in the Name of the Father, the Son, and the Holy Spirit. Amen.

*For binding prayers, name the emotion, the trial, the sin, the vice, etc. which is the issue. This also names the demon, because this is the effect they cause. For example, "spirit of restlessness, disobedience, greed, lying, bad friendships, lust, rebellion, curiosity, etc." You can also simply say "spirit of evil," but if a specific effect is the concern, it should be named. Prayer can be done in silence. Binding prayers should only be said over oneself and over a person who is under your authority, such as a child. "Indirect" binding prayers, where the wording indicates you are asking Our Lord to bind the demon, and not doing it yourself, may be said for anyone.

---

[1] http://www.sensustraditionis.org/Binding.pdf. By Fr. Chad Ripperger. Used with permission.

Consecration of One's Exterior Goods to the Blessed Virgin Mary

I, (Name), a faithless sinner, renew and ratify today in thy hands the vows of my Baptism; I renounce forever Satan, his pomps and works; and I give myself entirely to Jesus Christ, the Incarnate Wisdom, to carry my cross after Him all the days of my life, and to be more faithful to Him than I have ever been before. In the presence of all the heavenly court, I choose thee, O Mary, this day for my Mother and Mistress.

Knowing that I have received rights over all my exterior goods by the promulgation of the Natural Law by the Divine Author, I deliver and consecrate to thee, as thy slave, all of my exterior goods, past, present and future; I relinquish into thy hands, my Heavenly Mother, all rights over my exterior goods, including my health, finances, relationships, possessions, property, my job and my earthly success and I retain for myself no right of disposing the goods that come to me but leave to thee the entire and full right of disposing of all that belongs to me, without exception, according to thy good pleasure, for the greater glory of God in time and in eternity.

As I now interiorly relinquish what belongs to me exteriorly into thy hands, I entrust to thee the protection of those exterior goods against the evil one, so that, knowing that they now belong to thee, he cannot touch them. Receive, O good and pious Virgin, this little offering of what little is, in honor of, and in union with, that subjection which the Eternal Wisdom deigned to have to thy maternity; in homage to the power which both of you have over this poor sinner, and in thanksgiving for the privileges with which the Holy Trinity has favored thee.

Trusting in the providential care of God the Father and thy maternal care, I have full confidence that thou wilst take care of me as to the necessities of this life and will not leave me forsaken. God the Father, increase my trust in Thy Son's Mother; Our Lady of Fair Love, give me perfect confidence in the providence of Thy Son. Amen.[1]

---

[1] From "Deliverance Prayers: For Use by the Laity" by Fr. Chad Ripperger. Used with permission.

The Angelic Warfare Confraternity

The Angelic Warfare Confraternity was officially founded in 1727 by Pope Benedict XII. It unofficially began after the death of St. Thomas Aquinas, after whom it takes its inspiration. It is a Confraternity devoted to helping its members achieve chastity according to their state in life. Numerous saints have been members of this Confraternity, including St. Aloysius Gonzaga and Bl. Pier Giorgio Frassati.

As is stated on their website, "The Angelic Warfare Confraternity is a supernatural brotherhood or fellowship of men and women bound to one another in love and dedicated to pursuing and promoting chastity together under the powerful patronage St. Thomas Aquinas and the Blessed Virgin Mary. It is an official apostolate of the Dominican Order."

As is also indicated on their website,[1] where they answer common questions about the Confraternity and the blessed cord of St. Thomas Aquinas, this latter sacramental, with the attached blessing, is essentially a blessing of one's human sexuality.

In explaining this, they state:

> One's human sexuality consists of all those natural and personal instincts, desires, and emotions that tend toward love, relationships, marriage, and the procreation and education of children. This intimate structure within each of us is naturally a source of joy and new life for human beings. But on account of the wounds of original sin there is also a disturbance in our human sexuality. We are weak, vulnerable to temptation, and are prone to act on sexual impulses outside of the right time and place rather than to act in accord with wisdom and seek the higher good. When the priest blesses the cord and medal of St. Thomas, the priest says: "may all who wear these cords and medals be purified from all uncleanness of mind and body" and later on: "May the Lord gird you with the cincture of purity and by the merits of St. Thomas extinguish within you every evil desire…" Through the priest's words of blessing, the Spirit of Christ comes not only upon the cord and medal, but also to the person who will wear them. The Spirit comes to address the wounds of original sin as they afflict the man or woman's human sexuality. The Spirit comes to move the whole person down the often long road of healing, liberation, and growth in chastity.

---

[1] http://www.angelicwarfareconfraternity.org/catechesis-on-the-angelic-warfare-confraternity/

Addressing the question of the power of the blessing and sacramental, they state:

> The blessing is supernatural dynamite. Many people who go through ceremony and wear the blessed cord or medal testify to experiencing great relief from temptations and greater strength in resisting temptations. As St. Paul says, "the kingdom of God does not consist in talk, but in power" (1 Cor. 4:20).

Another effect from enrollment in the Confraternity involves the deeper spiritual connection to St. Thomas Aquinas, the merits of the Dominican Order, and the prayers of the other members of the Confraternity. As they state:

> St. Thomas Aquinas becomes an official personal patron of each Confraternity member, the treasure chest of graces merited by the Dominican Order is opened up to all in the Confraternity to draw upon, and the prayers of thousands of other members of the Confraternity come to the aid of all the other members every day. People often say they no longer feel isolated in the pursuit of chastity but tied to others in the same pursuit. They often say they feel stronger and more equipped for the struggle.

In the life of St. Thomas Aquinas, his early devotion to his religious vocation and to purity and chastity were greatly tested or, perhaps more fitting to say, assaulted by his family who opposed his decision. In their final desperate attempt to dissuade him from his vocation to the religious life, they imprisoned him and sent a prostitute into his room to seduce him. Immediately, he grabbed a bundle of burning twigs from the fireplace and chased the woman out of his room. After closing the door, he drew a Cross on the door with the smoldering twigs. At that moment, he fell into a vision, where two angels appeared to him and girded him with a cord around his waist and, in so doing, obtained for him the grace of perfect chastity.

This event was known to people in his day and, after his death, the cord was displayed for veneration. People touched cords of their own to this cord and wore them around their waists, in imitation of St. Thomas and seeking his intercession. The Church later instituted this Confraternity and also permitted the use of a medal which was printed to honor this angelic event and grace. Any Dominican priest, or a priest who has received permission from them, may enroll individuals in the Confraternity.

The Blessing on the Cord and Medal

Like the other sacramentals mentioned, the blessing of the cord and medal carry with it great protections from Our Lord. The blessing contains such wording as:

> "By means of the sacred cord of St. Thomas, grant to us who implore Your help through his intercession that we may successfully overcome the temptations of body and soul and come to be crowned with perpetual purity and integrity among the choirs of angels."

The Angelic Warfare Confraternity

Part of the blessing on the cord and medals says,

> "So that whoever reverently carries and wears them around his waist (bears and wears them) may be purified from all uncleanness of mind and body."

After the cord and medal have been presented to the individual, the priest says, among other things,

> "May the Lord gird you with the cincture of purity, and by the merits of St. Thomas Aquinas, extinguish within you every evil desire."

For those who are interested in enrolling in the Angelic Warfare Confraternity, speak to your pastor about doing so, or contact the Dominicans for more information.[2] Purity and chastity are virtues that every single Christian in all states of life must establish in order to protect the grace of salvation which Our Lord has bestowed upon us. To drive home this point, the words of St. Alphonsus Liguori are very helpful to reflect upon. He says,

> "Whenever the devil tempts us, let us place our entire confidence in the divine assistance, and let us recommend ourselves to Jesus Christ, and to the Most Holy Mary. We ought to do this particularly as often as we are tempted against chastity; for this is the most terrible of all temptations, and is the one by which the devil gains the most victories. We have not the strength to preserve chastity; this strength must come from God."[3]

He adds,

> "The occasion of sins of the flesh, in particular, is like a veil placed before the eyes, which prevents the soul from seeing either its resolutions, or the lights received from God, or the truths of eternity: in a word, it makes it forget everything, and almost blinds it."[4]

Membership in this Confraternity is a powerful weapon in our spiritual warfare arsenal. The intention of the Church in establishing this devotion (both the sacramental and the Confraternity) is to further bring about a healing of the wounds from sexual sin, a "renovation of the heart," and a "new innocence" by the working of the Holy Spirit and our cooperation with His activity and grace.

---

[2] AngelicWarfareConfraternity.org and https://www.awconfraternity.org/enroll
[3] *Preparation for Death*, 314
[4] *Preparation for Death*, 319

*Powerful Prayers
to
Our Lord
&
Our Lady*

Litany of the Most Precious Blood of Jesus

Lord, have mercy.
Christ, have mercy.
Lord, have mercy.
Christ hear us.
Christ graciously hear us.
God, the Father of Heaven, *have mercy on us.*
God, the Son, Redeemer of the world, *have mercy on us.*
God, the Holy Spirit, *have mercy on us.*
Holy Trinity, One God, *have mercy on us.*
Blood of Christ, only-begotten Son of the Eternal Father, *save us.*
Blood of Christ, Incarnate Word of God, *save us.*
Blood of Christ, of the New and Eternal Testament, *save us.*
Blood of Christ, falling upon the earth in the Agony, *save us.*
Blood of Christ, shed profusely in the Scourging, *save us.*
Blood of Christ, flowing forth in the Crowning with Thorns, *save us.*
Blood of Christ, poured out on the Cross, *save us.*
Blood of Christ, price of our salvation, *save us.*
Blood of Christ, without which there is no forgiveness. *save us.*
Blood of Christ, Eucharistic drink and refreshment of souls, *save us.*
Blood of Christ, stream of mercy, *save us.*
Blood of Christ, victor over demons, *save us.*
Blood of Christ, courage of Martyrs, *save us.*
Blood of Christ, strength of Confessors, *save us.*
Blood of Christ, bringing forth Virgins, *save us.*
Blood of Christ, help of those in peril, *save us.*
Blood of Christ, relief of the burdened, *save us.*
Blood of Christ, solace in sorrow, *save us.*
Blood of Christ, hope of the penitent, *save us.*
Blood of Christ, consolation of the dying, *save us.*
Blood of Christ, peace and tenderness of hearts, *save us.*
Blood of Christ, pledge of eternal life, *save us.*
Blood of Christ, freeing souls from purgatory, *save us.*
Blood of Christ, most worthy of all glory and honor, *save us.*
Lamb of God, who take away the sins of the world, *spare us, O Lord.*
Lamb of God, who take away the sins of the world, *graciously hear us, O Lord.*
Lamb of God, who take away the sins of the world, *have mercy on us.*
V. Thou hast redeemed us with Thy Blood, O Lord,
R. And made of us a kingdom for our God.

Slaying Dragons – Prepare for Battle

Let us pray.

Almighty and everlasting God, Who hast appointed Thine only-begotten Son to be the Redeemer of the world, and hast been pleased to be reconciled unto us by His Blood, grant us, we beseech Thee, so to venerate with solemn worship the price of our salvation, that the power thereof may here on earth keep us from all things hurtful, and the fruit of the same may gladden us for ever hereafter in heaven. Through the same Christ our Lord. Amen.

Novena to Our Lady, Undoer of Knots

1. Make the Sign of the Cross
2. Say the Act of Contrition. Ask pardon for your sins and make a firm promise not to commit them again.

Oh, my God, I am heartily sorry for having offended Thee. I detest all my sins because I dread the loss of Heaven and the pains of Hell. But most of all, because I offended Thee, my God, who art all good and deserving of all my love. I firmly resolve, with the help of Thy grace, to confess my sins, to do penance, and to amend my life. Amen

3. Say the first 3 decades of the Rosary.
4. Make the meditation of the day
5. Say the last 2 decades of the Rosary
6. Finish with the Prayer to Our Lady the Undoer of Knots

PRAYER TO MARY, UNDOER OF KNOTS (Closing Prayer)

Virgin Mary, Mother of fair love, Mother who never refuses to come to the aid of a child in need, Mother whose hands never cease to serve your beloved children because they are moved by the divine love and immense mercy that exists in your heart, cast your compassionate eyes upon me and see the snarl of knots that exist in my life.
You know very well how desperate I am, my pain and how I am bound by these knots.
Mary, Mother to whom God entrusted the undoing of the knots in the lives of His children, I entrust into your hands the ribbon of my life.
No one, not even the evil one himself, can take it away from your precious care. In your hands there is no knot that cannot be undone.
Powerful Mother, by your grace and intercessory power with Your Son and My Liberator, Jesus, take into your hands today this knot... [mention your intention] ...I beg you to undo it for the glory of God, once for all. You are my hope.
O my Lady, you are the only consolation God gives me, the fortification of my feeble strength, the enrichment of my destitution and with Christ the freedom from my chains.
Hear my plea.
Keep me, guide me, protect me, o safe refuge!

Mary, Undoer of Knots, pray for me

Slaying Dragons – Prepare for Battle

Meditation for Day 1
Dearest Holy Mother, Most Holy Mary, you undo the knots that suffocate your children, extend your merciful hands to me. I entrust to You today this knot... [mention your intention] ...and all the negative consequences that it provokes in my life. I give you this knot that torments me and makes me unhappy and so impedes me from uniting myself to You and Your Son Jesus, my Savior. I run to You, Mary, Undoer of Knots because I trust you and I know that you never despise a sinning child who comes to ask you for help. I believe that you can undo this knot because Jesus grants you everything. I believe that you want to undo this knot because you are my Mother. I believe that You will do this because you love me with eternal love.

Thank you, Dear Mother.
Mary, Undoer of Knots, pray for me.

The one who seeks grace, finds it in Mary's hands.

Meditation for Day 2
Mary, Beloved Mother, channel of all grace, I return to You today my heart, recognizing that I am a sinner in need of your help. Many times, I lose the graces you grant me because of my sins of egoism, pride, rancor and my lack of generosity and humility. I turn to You today, Mary, Undoer of knots, for You to ask your Son Jesus to grant me a pure, divested, humble and trusting heart. I will live today practicing these virtues and offering you this as a sign of my love for You. I entrust into Your hands this knot ... [mention your intention] ...which keeps me from reflecting the glory of God.

Mary, Undoer of Knots, pray for me.

Mary offered all the moments of her day to God.

Meditation for Day 3
Meditating Mother, Queen of heaven, in whose hands the treasures of the King are found, turn your merciful eyes upon me today. I entrust into your holy hands this knot in my life... [mention your intention] ...and all the rancor and resentment it has caused in me. I ask Your forgiveness, God the Father, for my sin. Help me now to forgive all the persons who consciously or unconsciously provoked this knot. Give me, also, the grace to forgive me for having provoked this knot. Only in this way can You undo it. Before You, dearest Mother, and in the name of Your Son Jesus, my Savior, who has suffered so many offenses, having been granted forgiveness, I now forgive these persons...and myself, forever. Thank you, Mary, Undoer of Knots for undoing the knot of rancor in my heart and the knot which I now present to you. Amen.

Mary, Undoer of Knots, pray for me.

Turn to Mary, you who desire grace.

Novena to Our Lady, Undoer of Knots

Meditation for Day 4

Dearest Holy Mother, you are generous with all who seek you, have mercy on me. I entrust into your hands this knot which robs the peace of my heart, paralyzes my soul and keeps me from going to my Lord and serving Him with my life. Undo this knot in my love... [mention your intention] ...O mother, and ask Jesus to heal my paralytic faith which gets down hearted with the stones on the road. Along with you, dearest Mother, may I see these stones as friends. Not murmuring against them anymore but giving endless thanks for them, may I smile trustingly in your power.

Mary, Undoer of Knots, pray for me.

Mary is the Sun and no one is deprived of her warmth.

Meditation for Day 5

Mother, Undoer of Knots, generous and compassionate, I come to You today to once again entrust this knot... [mention your intention] ...in my life to you and to ask the divine wisdom to undo, under the light of the Holy Spirit, this snarl of problems. No one ever saw you angry; to the contrary, your words were so charged with sweetness that the Holy Spirit was manifested on your lips. Take away from me the bitterness, anger and hatred which this knot has caused me. Give me, o dearest Mother, some of the sweetness and wisdom that is all silently reflected in your heart. And just as you were present at Pentecost, ask Jesus to send me a new presence of the Holy Spirit at this moment in my life. Holy Spirit, come upon me!

Mary, Undoer of Knots, pray for me.

Mary, with God, is powerful.

Meditation for Day 6

Queen of Mercy, I entrust to you this knot in my life... [mention your intention] ...and I ask you to give me a heart that is patient until you undo it. Teach me to persevere in the living word of Jesus, in the Eucharist, the Sacrament of Confession; stay with me and prepare my heart to celebrate with the angels the grace that will be granted to me. Amen! Alleluia!

Mary, Undoer of Knots, pray for me.

You are beautiful, Mary, and there is no stain of sin in You.

Meditation for Day 7
Mother Most Pure, I come to You today to beg you to undo this knot in my life... [mention your intention] ...and free me from the snares of Evil. God has granted you great power over all the demons. I renounce all of them today, every connection I have had with them and I proclaim Jesus as my one and only Lord and Savior. Mary, Undoer of Knots, crush the evil one's head and destroy the traps he has set for me by this knot. Thank you, dearest Mother. Most Precious Blood of Jesus, free me!

Mary, Undoer of Knots, pray for me.

You are the glory of Jerusalem, the joy of our people.

Meditation for Day 8
Virgin Mother of God, overflowing with mercy, have mercy on your child and undo this knot... [mention your intention] ...in my life. I need your visit to my life, like you visited Elizabeth. Bring me Jesus, bring me the Holy Spirit. Teach me to practice the virtues of courage, joyfulness, humility and faith, and, like Elizabeth, to be filled with the Holy Spirit. Make me joyfully rest on your bosom, Mary. I consecrate you as my mother, Queen and friend. I give you my heart and everything I have (my home and family, my material and spiritual goods.) I am yours forever. Put your heart in me so that I can do everything Jesus tells me.

Mary, Undoer of Knots, pray for me.

Let us go, therefore, full of trust, to the throne of grace.

Meditation for Day 9
Most Holy Mary, our Advocate, Undoer of Knots, I come today to thank you for undoing this knot in my life... [mention your intention] ...You know very well the suffering it has caused me. Thank you for coming, Mother, with your long fingers of mercy to dry the tears in my eyes; you receive me in your arms and make it possible for me to receive once again the divine grace. Mary, Undoer of Knots, dearest Mother, I thank you for undoing the knots in my life. Wrap me in your mantle of love, keep me under your protection, enlighten me with your peace! Amen.

Mary, Undoer of Knots, pray for me.

Little Rosary (or Chaplet) of Our Lady of Sorrows

~From The Glories of Mary, *by St. Alphonsus Liguori~*

V. Incline unto my aid, O God.
R. O Lord, make haste to help me.

Verse: My mother, enable my heart to share thy sorrow for the death of thy Son.
~or~

> My Mother! share thy grief with me,
> And let me bear thee company
> To mourn thy Jesus' death with thee.

First Dolor: The Prophecy of Simeon
Luke 2:25-35

I pity thee, O my afflicted Mother, on account of the first sword of sorrow that pierced thee, when in the temple, by the prophecy of St. Simeon, all the cruel sufferings that men would inflict on thy beloved Jesus were represented to thee, which thou hadst already learned from the holy Scriptures, even to his death before thy eyes upon the infamous wood of the cross, exhausted of blood and abandoned by all, and thou without the power to defend or relieve him. By that bitter memory, then, which for so many years afflicted thy heart, I pray thee, O my Queen, to obtain for me the grace that always in life and in death I may keep impressed upon my heart the passion of Jesus and thy sorrows.

Our Father, Seven Hail Mary, Glory be, and the Verse.

Second Dolor: The Flight into Egypt
Matthew 2:13-15

I pity thee, O my afflicted Mother, on account of the second sword that pierced thee when thou didst behold thy innocent Son, so soon after his birth, threatened with death by those very men for whom he had come into the world; so that thou wast obliged to flee with him by night secretly into Egypt. By the many hardships, then, that thou, a delicate young virgin, in company with thy exiled infant, didst endure in the long and wearisome journey through rough and desert countries, and in thy sojourn in Egypt, where, being unknown and a stranger, thou didst live all those years poor and despised, I pray thee O my beloved Lady, to obtain for me the grace to suffer with patience, in thy company till death, the trials of this miserable life, that I may be able in the next to be preserved from the eternal sufferings of hell deserved by me.

Our Father, Seven Hail Mary, Glory be, and the Verse.

Third Dolor: The Child Jesus is Lost in the Temple
Luke 2: 41-50

I pity thee, O my afflicted Mother, on account of the third sword that pierced thy heart at the loss of thy dear son, Jesus, who remained absent from thee in Jerusalem for three days, when not seeing thy beloved one by thy side, and not knowing the cause of his absence, I conceive, my loving queen, how in these nights thou didst not repose, and didst naught but sigh for him who was thy only good. By the sighs, then, of those three days, for thee so long and bitter, I pray thee to obtain for me the grace never to lose my God, that I may always live closely united to God, and thus united with him, depart from this world.

Our Father, Seven Hail Mary, Glory be, and the Verse.

Fourth Dolor: Mary meets Jesus on the Way of the Cross
Luke 23: 27-29

I pity thee, O my afflicted Mother, on account of the fourth sword that pierced thy heart, in seeing thy Jesus condemned to death, bound with ropes and chains, covered with blood and wounds, crowned with thorns, and falling under the weight of the heavy cross which he bore on his bleeding back when going like an innocent lamb to die for love of us. Thine eye then met his eye, and your glances were so many cruel arrows with which each wounded the loving heart of the other. By this great grief, then, I pray thee to obtain for me the grace to live wholly resigned to the will of my God, joyfully bearing my cross with Jesus to the last moment of my life.

Our Father, Seven Hail Mary, Glory be, and the Verse.

Fifth Dolor: Mary at the Foot of the Cross
John 19: 25-30

I pity thee, O my afflicted Mother, on account of the fifth sword that pierced thy heart, when on Mount Calvary thou didst behold thy beloved son, Jesus, dying slowly before thy eyes, amid so many insults, and in anguish, on that hard bed of the cross, without being able to give him even the least of those comforts which the greatest criminals receive at the hour of death. And I pray thee by the anguish which thou, oh my most loving mother, didst suffer together with thy dying Son, and by the tenderness thou didst feel, when, for the last time he spoke to thee from the cross, and taking leave of thee, left all of us to thee in the person of St. John, as thy children; and thou, still constant, didst behold him bow his head and expire; I pray thee to obtain for me the grace, by thy crucified love, to live and die crucified to everything in this world, in order to live only to God through my whole life, and thus to enter one day paradise, to enjoy him face to face.

Our Father, Seven Hail Mary, Glory be, and the Verse.

Little Rosary (or Chaplet) of Our Lady of Sorrows

Sixth Dolor: Mary receives the Body of Jesus from the Cross
John 19:39-40

I pity thee, O my afflicted Mother, on account of the sixth sword which pierced thy heart, when thou didst see the kind heart of thy Son pierced through and through after his death – a death endured fer those ungrateful men, who, even after his death, were not satisfied with the tortures they had inflicted upon him. By this cruel sorrow, then, which was wholly thine, I pray thee to obtain for me the grace to abide in the heart of Jesus, who was wounded and opened for me; in that heart, I say, which is the beautiful abode of love, where all the souls who love God repose; and that living there, I will never love or think of any thing but God. Most holy Virgin, thou canst do it; from thee I hope for it.

Our Father, Seven Hail Mary, Glory be, and the Verse.

Seventh Dolor: Mary watches as Jesus is laid in the Tomb
Luke 23: 50-56; John 19:39-42

I pity thee, O my afflicted Mother, on account of the seventh sword that pierced thy heart, on seeing in thy arms thy Son who had just expired, no longer fair and beautiful as thou didst once receive him in the stable of Bethlehem, but covered with blood, livid, and lacerated by wounds which exposed his very bones. My Son, thou saidst, my Son, to what has love brought thee? And when he was borne to the sepulchre, thou didst wish to accompany him thyself, and help to put him in the tomb with thy own hands; and, bidding him a last farewell, thou hast left thy loving heart buried with thy Son. By all the anguish of thy pure soul, obtain for me, oh mother of fair love, pardon for the offences that I have committed against my God, whom I love, and of which I repent with my whole heart. Wilt thou defend me in temptations? Assist me at the hour of my death, that, being saved by the merits of Jesus and thine, I may come one day with thy aid, after this miserable exile, to sing in paradise the praises of Jesus and thine through all eternity. Amen.

Our Father, Seven Hail Mary, Glory be, and the Verse.

V. Pray for us, O most sorrowful Virgin
R. That we may be worthy of the promises of Christ.

Let us pray.

O God, at whose passion, according to the prophecy of Simeon, the sword of sorrow pierced through the most sweet soul of the glorious virgin and mother, Mary, grant that we, who commemorate and reverence her dolors, may experience the blessed effect of thy passion, who livest and reignest world without end. Amen.

*Pope Benedict XIII granted many indulgences to this Chaplet to encourage its recitation and the meditation on the Sorrows of Our Lady. While these indulgences are no longer in effect in the post-conciliar age, the merit and spiritual fruitfulness of these prayers remains, as does the recommendation of many Saints to take up this devotion.

Chaplet of Our Lady of Sorrows

V: O God, come to my assistance
R: O Lord, make haste to help me
V: Glory be to the Father, and to the Son, and to the Holy Spirit,
R: As it was in the beginning, is now, and ever shall be, world without end. Amen.

The First Sorrow
The Presentation in the Temple (Prophecy of Simeon)

Sorrow as sharp as a sword shall pierce Mary's heart because of her Child. Mary is in the Temple, having come with Joseph to present the Child to God. They meet Simeon, the holy man, and Anna, the prophetess. Simeon takes the Baby in his arms, saying he will now die in peace because he has seen Christ, then he foretells the sorrow to come.

I grieve for you, O Mary, most sorrowful, in the affliction of your tender heart at the prophecy of the holy and aged Simeon. Dear Mother, by your heart so afflicted, obtain for me the virtue of humility and the gift of the holy fear of God.

Hail Mary…

The Second Sorrow
The Flight into Egypt

Soon the sword of sorrow strikes. Herod the King seeks to kill the Child. Warned in sleep by an angel, Joseph takes Jesus and His Mother Mary, setting out for Egypt, where they lived in obscurity and poverty until it was safe to return to Nazareth.

I grieve for you, O Mary most sorrowful, in the anguish of your most affectionate heart during the flight into Egypt and your sojourn there. Dear Mother, by your heart so troubled, obtain for me the virtue of generosity, especially toward the poor, and the gift of piety.

Hail Mary…

The Third Sorrow
The Loss of Jesus For Three Days

When Jesus is twelve, He is taken to Jerusalem for the Feast of Passover. On the return journey Joseph and Mary find at the end of the first day that Jesus is not with them. Racked with anxiety, they search for Him. Nobody in the streets, not even the beggars, can tell them where He is. Not till the third day do they find Him, in the Temple.

I grieve for you, O Mary most sorrowful, in those anxieties which tried your troubled heart at the loss of your dear Jesus. Dear Mother, by your heart so full of anguish, obtain for me the virtue of chastity and the gift of knowledge.

Hail Mary…

The Fourth Sorrow
The Way to Calvary

Mary has known fear and sorrow, but none so great as seeing her beloved Son stumbling under the weight of the Cross. She hears the jeering shouts from the crowd and has no power to help Him. Pity and love are in her eyes as she gazes at His blood-stained face. To many around her He is no better than a criminal, and her heart is breaking as she follows Him to Calvary or Golgotha.

I grieve for you, O Mary most sorrowful, in the consternation of your heart at meeting Jesus as He carried His cross. Dear Mother, by your heart so troubled, obtain for me the virtue of patience and the gift of fortitude.

Hail Mary…

The Fifth Sorrow
The Crucifixion

With John, Mary stands at the foot of the Cross. "A sword shall pierce thy soul," Simeon told her. Truly her heart is pierced with sorrow. Her beloved Son is dying and she shares in His suffering. She does not ask God to take away this agony. She is His Mother, so close to Him that His pain is hers, too. And now He speaks from the Cross: "Woman, behold thy son." Jesus give His Mother to John, and to us. For all eternity she is our Mother.

I grieve for you, O Mary most sorrowful, in the martyrdom which your generous heart endured in standing near Jesus in His agony. Dear Mother, by your afflicted heart, obtain for me the virtue of temperance and the gift of counsel.

Hail Mary…

Chaplet of Our Lady of Sorrows

The Sixth Sorrow
The Descent from the Cross

It is over. Dark clouds have appeared in the sky and upon the world. Jesus is dead. Joseph of Arimathea and Nicodemus take down the Body from the Cross. and Mary receives It in her arms. She is filled with a sadness that no human heart has known. This is her Son. Once she had cradled Him in her arms. listened to His voice, watched Him working at the carpenter's bench. Now He is dead. She does not weep; her grief is too great for tears.

I grieve for you, O Mary most sorrowful, in the wounding of your compassionate heart, when the side of Jesus was struck by the lance before His Body was removed from the cross. Dear Mother, by your heart thus transfixed, obtain for me the virtue of fraternal charity and the gift of understanding.

Hail Mary…

The Seventh Sorrow
The Burial of Jesus

Hastily the Body is wrapped in a clean linen cloth. Nicodemus has brought myrrh and aloes, and the Body is bound in the Shroud with them. nearby is a new tomb, belonging to Joseph of Arimathea, and there they lay Jesus. Mary and John and the holy women follow them and watch as the great stone to the sepulchre is rolled. it is the end.

I grieve for you, O Mary most sorrowful, for the pangs that wrenched your most loving heart at the burial of Jesus. Dear Mother, by your heart sunk in the bitterness of desolation, obtain for me the virtue of diligence and the gift of wisdom.

Hail Mary…

Prayers to Our Lady of Perpetual Succour

These prayers appear in the traditional collection of indulgenced prayers called The Raccolta. *These prayers, therefore, are ancient and beautiful. Many of them are still enriched with indulgences. They are all meritorious to obtain grace and the assistance of Heaven. There are three prayers, and they have been placed on separate pages for ease of use by the reader.*

I

Behold at thy feet, O Mother of Perpetual Succour, a wretched sinner who has recourse to thee, and confides in thee. O Mother of mercy, have pity on me. I hear thee called by all, the refuge and the hope of sinners: be, then, my refuge and my hope. Assist me, for the love of Jesus Christ; stretch forth thy hand to a miserable fallen creature who recommends himself to thee, and who devotes himself to thy service for ever. I bless and thank Almighty God, who in mercy has given me this confidence in thee, which I hold to be a pledge of my eternal salvation. It is true that in the past I have miserably fallen into sin, because I had not recourse to thee. I know that, with thy help, I shall conquer. I know, too, that thou wilt assist me, if I recommend myself to thee; but I fear that, in time of danger, I may neglect to call on thee, and thus lose my soul. This grace, then, I ask of thee, and this I beg, with all the fervour of my soul, that, in all the attacks of hell, I may ever have recourse to thee. O Mary, help me. O Mother of Perpetual Succour, never suffer me to lose my God.

II

O Mother of Perpetual Succour, grant that I may ever invoke thy most powerful name, which is the safeguard of the living and the salvation of the dying. O purest Mary! O sweetest Mary! let thy name henceforth be ever on my lips. Delay not, O blessed Lady, to succour me, whenever I call on thee; for, in all my temptations, in all my needs, I shall never cease to call on thee, ever repeating thy sacred name, Mary! Mary! Oh, what consolation, what sweetness, what confidence, what emotion fills my soul when I utter thy sacred name, or even only think of thee! I thank the LORD for having given thee, for my good, so sweet, so powerful, so lovely a name. But I will not be content with merely uttering thy name. Let my love for thee prompt me ever to hail thee Mother of Perpetual Succour.

Prayers to Our Lady of Perpetual Succour

III

O Mother of Perpetual Succour, thou art the dispenser of all the gifts which God grants to us miserable sinners; and for this end He has made thee so powerful, so rich, and so bountiful, in order that thou mayest help us in our misery. Thou art the advocate of the most wretched and abandoned sinners who have recourse to thee: come to my aid; I commend myself to thee. In thy hands I place my eternal salvation, and to thee I entrust my soul. Count me among thy most devoted servants; take me under thy protection, and it is enough for me. For, if thou protect me, I fear nothing; not from my sins, because thou wilt obtain for me the pardon of them; nor from the devils, because thou art more powerful than all hell together; nor even from Jesus, my Judge, because by one prayer from thee He will be appeased. But one thing I fear: that in the hour of temptation, I may through negligence fail to have recourse to thee, and thus perish miserably. Obtain for me, therefore, the pardon of my sins, love for Jesus, final perseverance, and the grace ever to have recourse to thee, O Mother of Perpetual Succour.

Reflection – Our Lady's Suffering, Love, and Power

In St. Alphonsus' Liguori's exemplary book on the Blessed Virgin Mary, *The Glories of Mary*, we learn more of what was stated by exorcists, such as Fr. Ripperger, in *Slaying Dragons*. Mary's role and influence in our spiritual lives is discussed in Chapter Ten, "Protecting Our Spiritual Lives." Here, the reader is presented with additional insights regarding Our Lady's suffering, love, and power to act upon our souls to aid us in our pursuit of holiness.

Mary, due to her election to be the Mother of God, and in particular through the sufferings she endured through her participation in her Son's sufferings, has merited a special role in the life of the faithful. This includes receiving special insights into God's plan and regarding what is happening in our spiritual lives with temptation and any extraordinary activity of the Evil One.

From *The Glories of Mary*, we learn:
- That Our Lady was enlightened early on through her knowledge of Sacred Scripture

"Already the most Blessed Virgin, as Saint Jerome says, was enlightened by the sacred Scriptures, and knew the sufferings that the Redeemer was to endure in His life, and still more at the time of His death."[1]

- That all the specific details of Our Lord's sufferings were revealed to Our Lady

"Mary, I say, already knew all these torments which her Son was to endure; but, in the words addressed to her by Simeon, 'And thy own soul a sword shall pierce,' all the minute circumstances of the sufferings, internal and external, which were to torment her Jesus in His Passion, were made known to her, as Our Lord revealed to St. Teresa. She consented to all with a constancy which filled even the angels with astonishment."[2]

- That the suffering Our Lady endured in her life, as a result of this knowledge of Our Lord's Passion, was never-ending

"But Saint Bernard affirms, speaking of the great sorrow which Mary experienced on this day, that from that time forward 'she died living, enduring a sorrow more cruel than death.' In every moment she lived dying; for in every moment she was assailed by the sorrow of the death of her beloved Jesus, which was a torment more cruel than any death."[3]

- That this illumination of Our Lady's intellect was by the Holy Spirit, giving her a knowledge of the Messiah's suffering that surpassed that of all the prophets

---

[1] St. Alphonsus Liguori, *The Glories of Mary*, 2nd Ed., edited by Fr. Robert A. Coffin, Burns and Oates Publisher, 1868, Pg. 360
[2] Ibid. pg. 361
[3] Ibid. pg. 365

The angel revealed to St. Bridget, "There can be no doubt, that, enlightened by the Holy Ghost in a far higher degree than all the prophets, she, far better than they, understood the predictions recorded by them in the sacred Scriptures concerning the Messias."[4]

- That Our Lady's sorrow was proportionate to her love for her Son, and thus, none have loved nor suffered as she

St. Alphonsus quotes Cornelius a Lapide as saying, "to understand the greatness of Mary's grief at the death of her Son, we must understand the greatness of the love she bore Him." Mary loved Our Lord as much as any creature is capable of loving Him. As such, there was no love like her love, and there was no sorrow like the sorrow which was hers.[5]

- That, when we meditate on Our Lady's sufferings, it is so pleasing to Our Lord that He grants special favors to us through His Mother's intercession

Our Lord revealed to Saint Elizabeth four principal graces that He would bestow on those who meditated on the sufferings of His Mother. Of those, notable here is the promise "that He would commit such devout clients to the hands of Mary, with the power to dispose of them in whatever manner she might please, and to obtain for them all the graces she might desire."[6]

- That, comforted beneath Our Lady's mantle as a result of accompanying her in her sufferings, we will be granted special protection against the activity of the diabolic

"This [desire to aid us] is exactly what Mary gave St. Gertrude to understand, when she showed herself to her with her mantle spread out to receive all who have recourse to her. At the same time, the Saint was told that 'Angels constantly guard the clients of this Blessed Virgin from the assaults of hell'."[7]

Let us, from the additional words of such great Saints, take courage and fly to Mary for help! She is a mighty advocate and the Queen of Heaven. Our Lord, whose love for her is incomprehensible to us, will grant all that she asks!

---

[4] Ibid. pg. 405
[5] Ibid. pg. 414
[6] Ibid. pg. 417
[7] Ibid. pg. 110

Sub Tuum Praesidium

We fly to thy patronage,
O holy Mother of God;
despise not our petitions in our necessities,
but deliver us always from all dangers,
O glorious and blessed Virgin.
Amen.

Our Lady of Sorrows, please obtain for me the grace to know the root causes of my struggles. Reveal to me which demon is the source for my spiritual disquiet; and then, O Virgin Most Powerful, please drive these, and all other malicious enemies, out of our lives. Amen.[8]

---

[8] Can be prayed on behalf of another person as well. "Demon" refers to the temptation or issue the demon is stirring up, not seeking the name of the demon.

Prayers to Prepare the Soul for Spiritual Warfare

Prayer for Perseverance in the Storm

O Mary, my tender Mother, and Comforter of the Afflicted, help me to see that Our Lord is indeed with me. We live, now, with Him asleep in this storm. We live, now, in the field sown, by an enemy, with weeds.

My dear Lady, Undoer of Knots, intercede for me and break the bonds of the enemy which oppress me in this darkness. Cover me with your protective mantle that, loving you and taking refuge in your Immaculate Heart, I may be shielded from the attacks of the evil one and rest in the peace and light of Our Lord.

O Mother of Sorrows, you know the plans that Our Lord has for His Church in these times. Obtain for me an increase in the gift of wisdom, that I may see as God sees, and persevere in grace by clinging to His Most Sacred Heart.

Place me gently in His arms, that I may rest there with confidence, and find peace knowing that He is with me, as He was with Peter, in the midst of the storms that seek to distract me from His Love. Amen[1]

---

[1] An original prayer by the author, composed while researching for *Slaying Dragons*. It is available as a printed holy card at www.TheRetreatBox.com

A Prayer to End an Oppression

Most Sacred Heart of Jesus, Most Immaculate Heart of Mary, I place my trust in you.
Virgin Most Powerful, pray for us.

In the Name of Jesus Christ, I command you, spirit of _____, to depart from me and leave me in peace, and I bind you and cast you to the foot of the Cross to be judged by Our Lord.

O Virgin Most Powerful, cast far away from me the evil spirits that seek to corrupt my trust in Our Lord, confuse my faith in His goodness and Providence, and weaken my love for Him.

Our Lady, Undoer of Knots, intercede for me and obtain for me freedom from any evil orchestrations. Break up any efforts of the evil one to [mention your dilemma or signs of oppression].

O Mother of Sorrows, you know the plans that Our Lord has for me. Help me to know them as well, and to follow them, and to trust that His love and Providence are guiding all events in my life. Let me rest with confidence in His arms, and find peace knowing that He is with me, as He was with Peter, in the midst of the storms that seek to distract me from His love.

O, Our Blessed Lady and Queen, protect me with your authority, and obtain for me, through your intercession with Our Lord, the grace to love Him well. Amen.[1]

---

[1] Another original prayer by the author, composed while researching for *Slaying Dragons*. It is available as a printed holy card at www.TheRetreatBox.com

Prayer to St. Joseph

From the encyclical of Pope Leo XIII, Quamquam Pluries, who encouraged its frequent recitation. It is enriched with a partial indulgence. The Holy Father also asked that it be added to the end of the Rosary, especially during the month of October, which is dedicated to the Rosary.

To you, O blessed Joseph, do we come in our tribulation, and having implored the help of your most holy spouse, we confidently invoke your patronage also.

Through that charity which bound you to the Immaculate Virgin Mother of God and through the paternal love with which you embraced the Child Jesus, we humbly beg you graciously to regard the inheritance which Jesus Christ has purchased by his Blood, and with your power and strength to aid us in our necessities.

O most watchful Guardian of the Holy Family, defend the chosen children of Jesus Christ;
O most loving father, ward off from us every contagion of error and corrupting influence;
O our most mighty protector, be kind to us and from heaven assist us in our struggle with the power of darkness.

As once you rescued the Child Jesus from deadly peril, so now protect God's Holy Church from the snares of the enemy and from all adversity; shield, too, each one of us by your constant protection, so that, supported by your example and your aid, we may be able to live piously, to die in holiness, and to obtain eternal happiness in heaven. Amen.

Prayer to Guardian Angel

Angel of God,
my Guardian dear,
to whom God's love
commits me here,
ever this day
be at my side
to light, to guard,
to rule, to guide.
Amen

St. Patrick's Breastplate

The Lorica of St. Patrick

I bind to myself today
The strong virtue of the Invocation of the Trinity:
I believe the Trinity in the Unity
The Creator of the Universe.

I bind to myself today
The virtue of the Incarnation of Christ with His Baptism,
The virtue of His crucifixion with His burial,
The virtue of His Resurrection with His Ascension,
The virtue of His coming on the Judgment Day.

I bind to myself today
The virtue of the love of seraphim,
In the obedience of angels,
In the hope of resurrection unto reward,
In prayers of Patriarchs,
In predictions of Prophets,
In preaching of Apostles,
In faith of Confessors,
In purity of holy Virgins,
In deeds of righteous men.

I bind to myself today
The power of Heaven,
The light of the sun,
The brightness of the moon,
The splendour of fire,
The flashing of lightning,
The swiftness of wind,
The depth of sea,
The stability of earth,
The compactness of rocks.

I bind to myself today
God's Power to guide me,

Slaying Dragons – Prepare for Battle

God's Might to uphold me,
God's Wisdom to teach me,
God's Eye to watch over me,
God's Ear to hear me,
God's Word to give me speech,
God's Hand to guide me,
God's Way to lie before me,
God's Shield to shelter me,
God's Host to secure me,
Against the snares of demons,
Against the seductions of vices,
Against the lusts of nature,
Against everyone who meditates injury to me,
Whether far or near,
Whether few or with many.

I invoke today all these virtues
Against every hostile merciless power
Which may assail my body and my soul,
Against the incantations of false prophets,
Against the black laws of heathenism,
Against the false laws of heresy,
Against the deceits of idolatry,
Against the spells of witches, and smiths, and wizards,
Against every knowledge that binds the soul of man.

Christ, protect me today
Against every poison, against burning,
Against drowning, against death-wound,
That I may receive abundant reward.

Christ with me, Christ before me,
Christ behind me, Christ within me,
Christ beneath me, Christ above me,
Christ at my right, Christ at my left,
Christ when I lie down,
Christ when I sit down,
Christ when I arise,
Christ in the heart of everyone who thinks of me,
Christ in the mouth of everyone who speaks to me,
Christ in every eye that sees me,
Christ in every ear that hears me.

St. Patrick's Breastplate

I bind to myself today
The strong virtue of an invocation of the Trinity,
I believe the Trinity in the Unity
The Creator of the Universe.

Act of Faith

O MY GOD, I firmly believe that Thou art one God in Three Divine Persons, Father, Son and Holy Ghost. I believe that Thy Divine Son became Man, and died for our sins, and that He will come to judge the living and the dead. I believe these and all the truths which the Holy Catholic Church teaches, because Thou hast revealed them, Who canst neither deceive nor be deceived.

Or

O my God, I firmly believe that You are one God in three divine Persons, Father, Son and Holy Spirit. I believe that Your divine Son became man and died for our sins, and that He will come to judge the living and the dead. I believe these and all the truths which the Holy Catholic Church teaches, because in revealing them You can neither deceive nor be deceived.

Litany of Humility

O Jesus, meek and humble of heart,   **... hear me.**
From the desire of being esteemed,   **... deliver me, Jesus.**
From the desire of being loved   **... deliver me, Jesus.**
From the desire of being extolled   **... deliver me, Jesus.**
From the desire of being honored   **... deliver me, Jesus.**
From the desire of being praised   **... deliver me, Jesus.**
From the desire of being preferred to others   **... deliver me, Jesus.**
From the desire of being consulted   **... deliver me, Jesus.**
From the desire of being approved   **... deliver me, Jesus.**
From the fear of being humiliated   **... deliver me, Jesus.**
From the fear of being despised   **... deliver me, Jesus.**
From the fear of suffering rebukes   **... deliver me, Jesus.**
From the fear of being calumniated   **... deliver me, Jesus.**
From the fear of being forgotten   **... deliver me, Jesus.**
From the fear of being ridiculed   **... deliver me, Jesus.**
From the fear of being wronged   **... deliver me, Jesus.**
From the fear of being suspected   **... deliver me, Jesus.**

That others may be loved more than I,   **... Jesus, grant me the grace to desire it.**
That others may be esteemed more than I   **... Jesus, grant me the grace to desire it.**
That, in the opinion of the world, others may increase and I may decrease   **... Jesus, grant me the grace to desire it.**
That others may be chosen and I set aside   **... Jesus, grant me the grace to desire it.**
That others may be praised and I unnoticed   **... Jesus, grant me the grace to desire it.**
That others may be preferred to me in everything   **... Jesus, grant me the grace to desire it.**
That others may become holier than I, provided that I may become as holy as I should   **... Jesus, grant me the grace to desire it.**

Parental Blessing of a Child

Father's Prayer of Blessing over Child[1]

I, your father, bless you in the name of our Father, God almighty, and by the authority given to me by God almighty over you, do hereby cast any and all evil spirits from you. In the name of the Father, and the Son, and the Holy Spirit. Amen

Mother's Prayer of Blessing over Child

By the authority given to me by your father, given to him by God Almighty over you, I, your mother, bless you in the name of the Father, and the Son, and the Holy Spirit. Amen

From *Slaying Dragons:*
"Parents can bless their children, tracing the Sign of the Cross with their thumb on the forehead of the child, and using a commanded prayer saying, "God bless you," and then a blessing is given."[2]

---

[1] From the *Five Stones to Freedom Prayer Card,* by Liber Christo. Used with permission.
[2] Pg. 93

Notes & Journaling

Notes

Slaying Dragons – Prepare for Battle

Notes

Slaying Dragons – Prepare for Battle

Notes

Slaying Dragons – Prepare for Battle

Notes

Slaying Dragons – Prepare for Battle

Notes

Slaying Dragons – Prepare for Battle

Notes

About the Author

Charles D. Fraune was the founding Theology teacher of Christ the King Catholic High School in Huntersville, NC and was a Theology teacher there for ten years. He left teaching on the high school level to found the *Slaying Dragons Apostolate* as a result of the response to his best-selling spiritual warfare book, Slaying Dragons: What Exorcists See & What We Should Know. This Apostolate is dedicated to sharing the wisdom of spiritual warfare from the counsel of modern exorcists in the context of the Church's two-thousand-year history of authoritative teaching on the subject.

In addition to the above, he has taught nearly every grade level, from second grade to adult, including on the college and Diocesan level. He spent three semesters in seminary with the Diocese of Raleigh at St. Charles Borromeo Seminary in Pennsylvania. This completed a nine-year discernment of the priesthood and religious life after which he discerned that Our Lord was not calling him to the priesthood. He has a Master of Arts in Theology from the Christendom College Graduate School, as well as an Advanced Apostolic Catechetical Diploma. His enjoyment of writing began over twenty years ago and culminated in his first completed book, Come Away By Yourselves, a guide to prayer for busy Catholics. He has also written a spiritual warfare manual for youth and their parents, called Swords and Shadows: Navigating Youth Amidst the Wiles of Satan.

Charles is also a dedicated "backyard farmer." He lives in the Diocese of Charlotte, NC with his wife and three young children.

To our readers

We would like to hear from our readers.

Comments, questions, suggested topics for additional books, etc.

Please send your email to CharlesFraune@TheRetreatBox.com.

Keep up with spiritual warfare news, commentaries, and publications at our website: www.TheSlayingDragonsBook.com.

Support this author's work by buying books directly from him, at www.TheRetreatBox.com

Support him on Patreon https://www.patreon.com/theslayingdragonsbook

This book is available in three editions: paperback, hardcover, and spiral bound. Please visit the above websites to learn more.